Wilderness Cuisine

How to Prepare and Enjoy
Fine Food on the Trail
and in Camp

Carole Latimer

♟ WILDERNESS PRESS

FIRST EDITION May 1991
Second printing May 1992
Third printing September 1996
Fourth printing April 1998
Fifth printing June 2000

Copyright © 1991 by Carole Latimer
Cover and illustrations by Jon Larson
Book design by Roslyn Bullas

Library of Congress Card Catalog Number 91-9288
International Standard Book Number 0-89997-114-8

Manufactured in the United States of America

Published by **Wilderness Press**
       1200 5th Street
       Berkeley, CA 94710
       (800) 443-7227; FAX (510) 558-1696
       mail@wildernesspress.com
       www.wildernesspress.com

Contact us for a free catalog

Printed with soy-based ink

Library of Congress Cataloging-in-Publication Data

Latimer, Carole.
        Wilderness cuisine : how to prepare and enjoy fine food on the trail and in camp /
Carole Latimer.
        p.   cm.
        Includes index.
        ISBN 0-89997-114-8
        1. Outdoor cookery. I. Title
TX823.L37 1991
641.5'78—dc20   91-9288
                                           CIP

To
Peggy and Bill Latimer
and
Hope McGrath

Contents

Acknowledgments

Many years of cooking for people who come on Call of the Wild wilderness trips are behind this book, so my thanks are not only to people who have helped with *Wilderness Cuisine*, but also to those who have in one way or another helped me keep my business going since 1978.

What would we do without a little help from our friends? Thanks for inspiration, encouragement and material support from my dear friends Anne Dowie, Hjordis Fammestad, Lyn Alford, Katy Raddatz, and Judith Calson.

I thank my father Bill Latimer for sharing his love of the wilderness with me, and my mother Peggy Latimer for teaching me to appreciate good food—her home-canned goods and fresh produce from my folks' garden and orchard are greatly appreciated on wilderness trips.

Thank you Hope McGrath, my staunch friend and wise guardian angel for 20 years, for nurturing my creativity and believing in me.

Dixie Mitchell-Clow got me to start writing this book by sitting down at the computer and saying "Talk to me." *Mahalos* to John Ono who not only contributed his considerable knowledge of food, but cooked my meals and generally kept my life together so I could finish it.

Winter survival expert David Beck lent his knowledge on hypothermia and dehydration. Nutritionist and exercise physiologist Tacy Weeks helped with the nutrition chapter. Workers at the Berkeley REI and North Face stores answered questions about equipment. Roslyn Bullas at Wilderness Press did a fine job of typesetting and design, and made sure the recipes were clear and consistent. Wilderness Press publisher and my editor Tom Winnett is a man of infinite patience and understanding.

Other friends in the Call of the Wild *calabash* who richly deserve my special thanks are Donna Behrens, Jenny Felmley, Kim Hall, Karen Anderson, Dotty Dennis and her sled dogs, Barbara Lipson, Madeline Martell, Jan Alcock, Burr Snider, Kate Coleman, the late Eric Shaefer, Gretchen Schneider, Joanie Dempsey, Marty Ellsworth Doub, Beo and Shenka, my sister JoAnne Latimer Rogers, and my brother Bill Latimer—who has steadfastly encouraged me to do what I love. And many, many thanks to all the women who have come on my wilderness trips, especially those who said "Seriously now, you should write a cookbook."

Introduction

I've been cooking for people who come on wilderness trips with my company, Call of the Wild, for over a dozen years, and have been camping and backpacking all my life. At age 7, I went on my first long backpacking trip. My father and I hiked over 11,400-foot Piute Pass in the Sierra carrying old army packboards, and ate fresh eggs, bacon, salads, golden trout. Dad even turned out beautiful golden-brown biscuits baked in a reflector oven. I guess that's what got me started.

I've always eaten well on backpacking trips, and you can too. My repertoire of recipes has expanded considerably over the years, and the recipes in this book reflect food trends from the health-food-conscious seventies to the California Cuisine movement of the nineties. You'll find recipes here for familiar old favorites like beans and rice, macaroni and cheese. Ethnic foods are represented, too. There are recipes for Thai, Mexican, Chinese, and Cajun food, and I've even included directions for preparing a Japanese sushi dinner on the trail. But, as you will see, making these exotic dishes isn't really hard.

The first chapter takes you through supermarkets, gourmet and health-food stores, and Indian, Thai and Chinese grocery stores and tells you about lightweight, non-perishable foods you can find there that are perfectly suited for backpacking.

Whatever your backpacking or camping style, there should be something for everyone here, from Spartan peakbaggers to romantic gourmets. Foods run the gamut from sensible and nutritious bulgur wheat to extravagantly delicious smoked salmon. Pesto, polenta, and sun-dried tomatoes are almost ideal backpacking foods, and there are several easy-to-make recipes using these "gourmet" food items.

You can eat like royalty in the backcountry and you don't have to be a gourmet cook. Cooking outdoors on a backpacking stove becomes easy with a little practice, and your success depends far more on pre-trip planning and preparation than on your skills as a chef.

Unlike the freeze-dried and other pre-packaged meals marketed to backpackers and campers, the recipes here won't give you second-class imitations, but really fine food. The reason is that the first principle of this book is to use fine, high-quality ingredients and fresh food whenever possible.

Over the years I've developed a good packing system and have devised effective ways for keeping food fresh without refrigeration. You can keep certain vegetables, including salad greens, fresh for several days. I'll tell you how.

You can bake on a backpacking stove, too. *Eggplant Parmesan, Andouille and Summer Garden Stew with Polenta, Strawberry Shortcake*, brownies and biscuits —these are just a few of the tasty and elegant dishes you can cook on the trail.

For people who are going on longer trips and want to travel very light, there's a chapter on home-drying food. Drying my own food with a home dehydrator has been especially fun and creative. You may be surprised at how easy it is—and at how good home-dried food can taste.

Backcountry cooking is both fun and rewarding. It can be as easy as boiling water for a simple meal of pasta with pesto, or as fancy as a chef's elaborate four-course creation including fresh baked cornbread and flaming *Cherries Jubilee*.

I've taken hundreds of people on wilderness trips. They've taught me that a wilderness party travels on its stomach. There's no better morale booster at the end of a day on the trail than a hearty, delicious meal. At mealtime tired bodies regain energy, spirits are rejuvenated, and laughter and lively conversation begin to flow. Good food helps bond people together and adds greatly to the success of your backpacking trip.

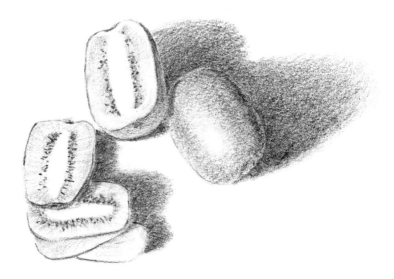

1

The Backpacker's Groceries

Over the years I've enjoyed discovering new foods for backpacking, and have looked at the cuisines of other countries for ideas to put variety into my menus. This chapter guides you through gourmet and health-food stores, supermarkets, and Chinese, Indian, and Thai grocery stores, and tells you about foods you can find there that are well-suited for backpacking. If you want to know more about any of the foods mentioned, check the glossary and also the index for recipes using these foods. If what you want isn't available in your area, check *Mail-Order Sources* at the back of the book.

Ethnic Markets

If you're lucky enough to live in an area with an ethnic population large enough to support a Chinese, Middle Eastern, Japanese, Indian, or Thai grocery store, you should take advantage of it and visit the store before your next backpacking trip. It's a good idea to make sure you actually like the taste of some of these exotic foods before going off to the wilderness. And if you're allergic to MSG, be sure to check the ingredients on the label before buying.

Chinese

One of the best things I've ever done to expand my knowledge of good food for backpacking trips is to take Martin Yan's walking tour of San Francisco

Chinatown. This famous chef is every bit as charming as he appears to be on his "Yan Can Cook" show on TV. He enthusiastically pointed out many things in Chinatown I could use for backpacking trips. One thing I noticed over and over again is how much cheaper food is in any Chinatown. But don't think you have to go all the way to a Chinatown to get some of the foods listed below—many are available in the Asian section of your local supermarket.

Grocery stores in Chinatown have a section of unrefrigerated meats with small packages of vacuum-packed ham and bacon. The meats are cured in soy sauce and are salty but tasty. These stores also have that wonderful Westfield Virginia-smoked ham, and you can buy it by the slice. Beef jerky can be found in Chinatown and it's much less expensive than jerky found in grocery stores. It does have a slightly different taste, so be sure to try it before buying a big supply.

San Francisco Chinatown has a sausage factory that makes hard, partly-dehydrated sausages that last two to three weeks without any refrigeration. They can be added to rice or soups, or eaten on the trail as a snack.

Everyone is familiar with soy sauce, and you might want to try Tamari, a special kind of soy sauce. Also be sure to try Oriental sesame oil. Its smoky taste is delicious in soups, stir fries and even grain salads. Fresh or candied ginger can be used to spice all kinds of dishes, and it also makes a warming tea that settles an upset stomach. Don't miss the delicious instant soups by Kikkoman: egg flower, shrimp, hot and sour, and several kinds of miso. You'll also find a wide selection of exotic sauces. Plum sauce gives added zest to meats; oyster sauce gives an authentic Chinese taste to stir-fried vegetables. Black-bean and chili pastes are extremely versatile. They can be used as condiments or added to rice, pasta, or many soups for flavor. Again, be sure to try these ahead of time to make sure you like them.

Try Marukan rice vinegar. It's diluted with water to only 4.1% acidity (most vinegars are 5-6% acidity), and a little sugar and salt are added. Use it in cooking and as a salad dressing. People are surprised to find that it doesn't need anything else with it to make a wonderful salad dressing, not even oil. Marukan rice vinegar is widely available in California supermarkets and health-food stores, too.

Be sure to check out the pasta section in Chinese grocery stores. Many Asian pasta varieties don't take as long to cook as Italian pasta and therefore are better for cooking at high elevations. People with wheat allergies will appreciate the pastas made from bean and rice flour. And don't forget about the backpacker's favorite instant meal: Top Ramen. It's found in almost infinite variety in Chinese grocery stores.

Bean curd is best known by its Japanese name, tofu. The dried bean curd sold in Chinatown produce markets is a good, lightweight source of protein for backpackers. It comes in flat sheets, needs no refrigeration, and must be rehydrated before it's cooked.

Indian   A trip to an Indian grocery store is great fun: the exotic aromas alone make it worth it. You can buy all kinds of spices in small amounts at reasonable prices: curry, cumin, cinnamon sticks, cayenne, saffron, pepper, and paprika to name just a few. There are also curry sauce mixes in small boxes and curry pastes which can be used as a base for a quick curry dish.

You'll find good deals on Indian tea, too. (For backpacking, it's best to buy tea in tea bags rather than loose tea.)

Take a look at the curry-snacks section. Curry snacks are an exotic version of the Wheat Chex-pretzels party mix that your Aunt Helen used to make, only they're made with ingredients like mung beans, peas, and lentils. Some are hot, so taste them first.

You can buy fragrant Basmati rice at bargain prices, and several kinds of lentils. The small, quick-cooking orange lentils are perfect for backpacking. They cook in about 15 minutes at sea level, and I've cooked them in about a half-hour at 8000 feet. They're apricot-colored and are called *Masoor Dahl*. The yellow lentils cook fairly quickly, too, but not as fast as the orange ones.

If you're planning on a longer trip in a warm climate you might want to try ghee. Ghee is clarified butter, used extensively in India because it keeps for long periods in hot weather without turning sour and can be heated to higher temperatures than butter without burning.

You'll also find peanuts, dried coconut, pistachios and all kinds of chutneys. Browse and ask the Indian clerk for help—you'll learn a lot by asking.

Thai

With the recent influx of Thai immigrants to the U.S., Thai restaurants and grocery stores are cropping up in many cities. It's an old and sophisticated cuisine that has much to offer backpackers. If you're unfamiliar with Thai food, try eating at a Thai restaurant. The Thai grocery store I shop at has recipes available for the uninitiated, and you'll a find a couple of Thai recipes in this book.

The Thai version of Top Ramen is very inexpensive, and you can get the noodles in wheat or rice with several different soup-mix bases. My favorite is the lemongrass-flavored Tom Yum base, but you may want to refrain from adding the little packet of hot sauce.

As with Chinese grocery stores, Thai groceries have lots of quick-cooking pastas (try the long "rice stick" noodles) and savory sauces. Thai chili paste is outstanding. It's especially good in soups or on noodles—or even spread on crackers.

If you're feeling adventurous, check out the Thai deli and ask the clerk about the prepared snacks you'll find there. Wonderful Thai jerky, unusual sweets made with coconut, and other exotic goodies that keep without refrigeration can be a good addition to your trip.

One real prize to be found in Thai markets is powdered coconut milk. It's lightweight and when mixed with water tastes like real coconut milk. Add it to curries and soups, use in desserts or combine with powdered juice mixes for a tropical drink.

Some of the Thai sweet soy mixes make a good marinade for beef jerky. Lemongrass, available fresh or dried, can be made into a tea and is an essential ingredient in the delicious Thai soup recipe found on page 152. Canned whole baby corn from Thailand is a special treat good in soups, salads, or stir fries. Some of the ingredients in Thai recipes may sound strange, but don't let that scare you off. Things like Nam Pla (fish sauce), lime leaves, and galanga root (similar to ginger) are easy to use and you'll get delicious results. Moreover, the Thai people working in the grocery store will give you lots of friendly help.

Health-Food Stores

Your health-food store may be the best all-round place to shop for food for your backpacking trip. If you're going on a long or strenuous backpacking trip you'll be especially interested in buying some of the nutrition-packed food found in health-food stores.

The bulk-food section alone could almost supply an entire trip. The health-food store I shop at sells 10 kinds of trail mix and 19 types of granola in bulk, and there are bins full of everything from high quality dried fruit, pastas, cereals and nuts to powdered milk, protein drinks, and vegetable bouillion.

Some grains sold in bulk that cook in under 20 minutes (a bit more at altitude) are couscous, white

rice, kasha, quinoa and bulgur wheat. The packaged quick-cooking grains and cereals found in
health-food stores are an even better idea for backpacking: brown rice that cooks in just 12 minutes,
instant polenta, quick-cooking barley-oat bran cereal—the list goes on and on.

There are packaged mixes of hummus, tabouli,
Nature's Burger, instant mashed potatoes
(Barbara's is one of the best), falafel, and all kinds
of quick pilaf mixes using rice, couscous, or bulgur
wheat as a base.

I don't like most of the instant dinners available at
regular supermarkets, but some of their counter-
parts sold at health-food stores taste pretty good.
My favorite brand, Fantastic Foods, has dishes like
Mandarin Chow Mein, Creamy Stroganoff and
Tofu Scrambler. You add tofu and they cook in 10
to 15 minutes. Fantastic Foods also makes wonderful instant refried bean mixes, one made with black
beans and one with pintos, and they can be turned
into soup, too. A health-food store is the best place
to buy all kinds of soup mixes—everything from
instant miso to cream of mushroom. They taste
better than the kinds commonly found in supermarkets and they're better for you. Mayacamas is
an especially good tasting brand and most of their
soup-mix packets also give tips for using them as
sauces in other recipes.

Herb teas are great on backpacking trips, when we
need to be consuming lots of liquids. Celestial Seasonings has a wide selection of teas. Some of my
favorites are Sleepy Time, Lemon Zinger, Red
Zinger, Cranberry Cove, and Raspberry Patch.
Pompadour, another favorite brand imported from
Germany, makes excellent mint and chamomile,
and a tasty three-fruits tea. Ginseng tea, which
many people feel is warming and energizing, is
found in health-food stores in many strengths, varieties—and prices.

Your health-food store is also a good place to stock up on quick energy goodies like granola bars, pemmican, carob- or yogurt-covered nuts, candy bars and cookies.

Tahini (sesame seed butter) and all kinds of nut butters (cashew, almond, peanut) are commonly found in health-food stores; spread them on the whole grain crackers and breads you'll find there too—you'll be carrying far more nutrition per ounce than with white bread or some of the more popular mass-produced crackers. Whole-wheat pastas are here, too. Check the cooking times, though—they often take longer to cook than the white-flour type.

Health-food stores carry tofu in several forms suitable for backpacking: powdered mix, vacuum packed, dried, or smoked (it's good; it tastes like cheese). And you haven't lived until you've tried tofu jerky. It may sound more like a line from a Woody Allen movie than something good to eat, but there actually is such a thing as tofu jerky and it's absolutely delicious. Tofu jerky is made by Wildwood Natural Foods and comes from—where else—Marin County, California.

Finally, don't forget those old health-food favorites: miso, TVP (textured vegetable protein), nutritional yeast, and wheat germ. If you've never used these foods, don't be put off by their "health nut" reputation. They can be used to boost the nutritional value of quick-cooking trail foods and keep you healthy and full of energy on long backpacking trips.

Gourmet Shops

You'll pay higher prices at gourmet shops, but since we expend more calories and less cash than usual when backpacking, I think there's no harm in splurging a bit on food. There are other good reasons for spending a little more on gourmet food. It's fun, high quality, and a wonderful taste treat after a long hike. In addition, because much of it is imported it travels well, needs no refrigeration, and can often go directly from the store right into your pack without being repackaged.

It would be impossible to cover everything you might find at your local gourmet shop, but here are a few of the foods I've enjoyed. Many of the cookies are terrific. If you've never tried biscotti, go for it. These Italian cookies are lightweight and sturdy and amazingly good. Candies, too: imported chocolate, English toffee and licorice, and little tin boxes of hard, fruit-flavored candies which always seem to taste especially good at high altitude.

Retort-packaging of foods is a vacuum packaging method that has been used in Europe for years and is beginning to catch on in this country. Retort-packaged foods keep for up to two years with no refrigeration. I once had a retort-packaged pizzalike bread imported from Italy that we heated in its package, and it tasted fresh-baked. Also look for tortellini, gnocchi and chicken cacciatore retort dishes in the gourmet shop.

Browse around for other things like dried mushrooms, canned pâtés, crackers, olive oil, fancy mustards, vinegars (balsamic, raspberry), cornichons, olives (calamata, Nicoise), maple syrup, jellies (jalapeño jelly is wonderful with cream cheese), sun-dried tomatoes, concentrated Italian tomato paste (it comes in a tube), instant polenta, and mixes for potato pancakes, crêpes, cornbread and muffins.

Delis and Specialty Stores

If you're pressed for time, a stop at your local deli can be a life saver. You could make your first night's meal from items purchased there. One warning: you should repackage deli items into containers that won't leak, or at least triple-bag them in ziploc bags. I guarantee you that the plastic containers supplied by the deli will leak.

Pasta

Try fresh pasta and pesto sauce (made with garlic, olive oil, basil, pine nuts, and Parmesan cheese).

Pesto may be the world's best backpacking food. You can eat it on pasta, rice, bread or baked potatoes, and it adds zing to soups and eggs. It keeps for days, and garlic is reputed to be a natural mosquito repellent!

Meat

You'll find a variety of hams, prosciutto, Canadian bacon, pancetta (Italian bacon), and many kinds of salami and sausages that with proper care will keep for several days without refrigeration. Avoid sausages made with poultry—they won't keep long; dry sausages such as linguisa, chorizo, pepperoni and Andouille are good choices.

Cheese

You can find all the cheese you need at the supermarket but you'll find more selection and better-tasting products at a cheese specialty store. Try a good freshly ground Parmesan cheese rather than the supermarket stuff that comes in the glow-green cardboard shaker. You won't need to bring as much because it's stronger—and the taste is incomparable.

Hard and dry cheeses are perfect for backpacking: Swiss, Jarlsberg, Gruyere, Parmesan, Romano, Reggiano. Try dry jack; this is not the softer white Monterey Jack cheese most of us are familiar with. Pale yellow and full of flavor, dry jack is a hard cheese with a black wax coating and keeps without refrigeration for a long time.

I'm not sure why, but smoked cheeses seem to hit the spot when you're camping. Edam and Gouda cheeses, plain or smoked, are wonderful and stay fresh in their red wax wrapping. For a special treat, try aged Gouda. It's a harder cheese than regular Gouda and has a strong, nutty flavor that is incredibly good.

Good old standbys like Monterey Jack and cheddar are fine trail cheeses too. You might also want to try some of the low-fat varieties that have come out in recent years.

You can take soft cheese if you eat it within the first couple of days. Make your first lunch on the trail a special little feast with Brie, Camembert, or Gorgonzola (a rich blue cheese) accompanied with apples, a good dark bread and calamata olives. Goat cheese is not for everyone, but for those who appreciate it, a sandwich made from a fresh baguette, goat cheese and *Herbed Sun-Dried Tomatoes in Olive Oil* (page 181) is heavenly.

The Super-market

If you live in an area where supermarkets have become huge food palaces with their own delicatessen, health-food, gourmet, and international sections, you can shop at your supermarket for foods like those listed above. But you can easily supply your trip with food purchased at an ordinary supermarket, too. Dried fruit, butter, eggs, cheese, powdered milk, crackers, cereal, oil, fresh produce, rice, and pastas are just a few of the more obvious staples. Listed below are some foods I regularly use on my backpacking trips that can be found in almost any supermarket; I've included the brand names I'm partial to as well.

Pastas: Macaroni and corkscrew pasta travel well. Capellini (also called Angel hair pasta) cooks fastest. Corn elbow macaroni is great with chili. Top Ramen

Grains: Ala (made by Krusteaz)—this is bulgur wheat—the pilaf and tabouli recipes are excellent. Minute Rice, Alber's cornmeal

Dried fruit: Sunsweet Premium Prunes (they come in an 8-oz can)

Powdered Drinks: Tang, Gatorade, Crystal Light, Wyler's, Milkman powdered milk, Swiss Miss Hot Chocolate, Saco powdered buttermilk

Tea: Twinings Tea—English Breakfast, Earl Grey, Black Currant, Darjeeling

Soup: Knorr and Mayacamas soup mixes, Knorr chicken, beef and vegetable bouillon cubes

Candy: Snickers, Heath Bars, Peanut Butter Cups, M&Ms

Cookies: Pepperidge Farm cookies, Fig Newtons, ginger snaps, Graham crackers

Canned Fish: Always buy better brands—canned fish of inferior quality can be really terrible. Sardines (Tiny Tots), Kipper Snacks, salmon,

albacore tuna or bonita, clams (Gorton's or
Snows), oysters, smoked oysters or clams (Reese,
Geisha), crab (Crown-Prince), shrimp (Geisha or
Orleans)

Meats: Swanson's canned chicken, Swanson's
canned turkey, canned hams (very small size),
Canadian bacon, Gallo dry salami

Condiments: Marukan rice vinegar, Grey Poupon
Dijon mustard, Tabasco sauce, Major Grey's
chutney, Bacos (bacon-flavored soy protein)

Instant Cereals: Cream of Wheat, Quaker Oatmeal

Cold Cereals: granola, Familia, Swiss Muesli,
Grapenuts

Spreads: Real butter (salted), Philadelphia Cream
Cheese, Kraft Cracker Barrel Cheese (comes in
small foil-wrapped bars)

Miscellaneous:
Krusteaz pancake mix
Lawry's tostada tortilla shells (well-packaged,
dry, keep indefinitely)
Small cans of salsa (7 oz)
Contadina tomato paste (6 oz)
Crushed pineapple (small can)
Instant mashed potatoes (brands without
additives taste best, such as Barbara's)
Popcorn
Maple syrup
Sugar cubes

Some of the foods listed above are processed foods.
I definitely make a few compromises for the sake of
ease of preparation and quicker cooking times
when backpacking, but in general I try to avoid
processed food. I don't like the taste of most mass-
produced quick meals and mixes sold in supermarkets. They satisfy neither the body nor the soul, and
if you don't eat this kind of food at home, there's no
reason to eat it when you're camping. I do not
subscribe to the theory that everything tastes better
outdoors. A boxed instant dinner loaded with salt,
additives and fake cheese tastes terrible wherever
it is eaten, and leaves you feeling empty.

You can make simple, delicious dishes from the
recipes in this book without using packaged gra-
vies, powdered butter (carry real butter or clarified
butter—it's well worth it), powdered pesto (truly
awful), or other fake sauces. The canned and retort

meals available in most supermarkets are not very good either. Usually one sample of a brand can give you a pretty good idea of what the other dishes in the line taste like. Try the food before your trip, and see what you think. And remember, the taste of processed food does not improve with exposure to fresh air.

Outdoor Stores

The food department of a well-stocked outdoor store sells everything from freeze-dried food to dehydrated honey and smoked salmon fillets. You can buy shortbread in tins, and fancy imported candies, and outdoor stores are the only place I've ever been able to find the mountain climber's favorite candy, Kendal Mint Cake.

You'll also find electrolyte replacement drinks, pemmican, and other high-energy bars (PowerBars are excellent), retort meals and instant soups. Soup Today makes individual cup servings of soup, and it isn't bad for an instant soup.

Outdoor stores also carry groceries you can buy in a supermarket, but sell them in very small quantities such as a selection of six Twining teabags, coffee bags, spiced cider. You can buy things like instant oatmeal, Swiss Miss (hot chocolate) and Milkman (dry milk) by the packet. You pay more buying food like this, but if you'll use only a couple of packages of Milkman, it may make sense to buy at the higher price per package rather than spending $6 on a big box of 12 quart packages you won't use.

Freeze-dried Food

Although you can put together better-tasting meals with higher nutrition than you'll get in a prepackaged freeze-dried meal, I think that freeze-dried food does have its place. It is, of course, indispensable to really heavy-duty climbing expeditions. And if you're going on a longer trip and want to keep both pre-trip prep and camp cooking to a minimum, you may want to plan one or two nights of freeze-dried meals. They always come in handy for that night you arrive in camp later than expected or when it rains at dinnertime. Just be aware that freeze-dried food is expensive. In the early 1990s a freeze-dried meal with two servings cost around $6—and I think one hungry backpacker can polish off two servings in no time.

In my opinion, AlpineAire is the best tasting of the freeze-dried food brands. They use brown rice, couscous, wild rice, and whole wheat pastas in some of their entrees, and they don't add preservatives, MSG, or artificial flavors. Desserts like chocolate pudding and blueberry-fruit cobbler are good, too.

The best way to use freeze-dried food, however, is to buy it packaged as individual items (not ready-to-serve combinations) and enliven the taste with your own spices and extra touches like real butter, fresh garlic, or a shot of sherry. Brown rice, lentils, pinto and navy beans, tomato flakes, onions, beef, chicken, turkey, clams, shrimp, celery, bell peppers, mixed vegetables, and mushrooms are just a few of the individually packaged items available. Even though I home-dry my own food, I use some freeze-dried food on longer trips. Peas and corn are better freeze-dried than home-dried, and freeze-dried eggs taste better than commercially dehydrated eggs. Freeze-dried potatoes rehydrate and cook much faster than dehydrated potatoes, too.

You can combine freeze-dried food and long-lasting fresh food for a delicious result, and you can substitute freeze-dried food for dried food in any of the recipes in this book. Plan in advance, and if your outdoor store doesn't carry what you need, you can mail-order freeze-dried food directly from the company.

2

Good Nutrition, Good Food, and the Backpacker's Appetite

As the official cook on Call of the Wild wilderness trips, I'm a long-time observer of backpacker's eating habits. The backcountry cook should know the facts about dehydration, hypothermia, and the effects of altitude. And before you start planning your menu, there are some things you should know about what backpackers like to eat and their nutritional needs.

Carbo-hydrates

First and foremost, backpackers crave carbohydrates—especially complex carbohydrates. On the trail, we eat huge amounts of bread, pasta, potatoes, and grains. Our bodies tell us to eat things like oatmeal at breakfast, baked potatoes at lunch, breads for snacks, and huge pasta dinners.

We crave simple carbos, too—dried fruit, honey, candy, jam. People who seldom eat candy find that they like sugar when backpacking. The surge of energy you get from simple carbohydrates feels great when you're carrying a pack up a steep trail. When choosing simple carbohydrates, some athletes think they perform better when they eat fructose sugars instead of glucose sugars. They feel fructose gives quick energy without the "crash" you feel when your blood sugar dives after eating a candy bar containing sucrose sugars, such as honey or corn syrup. Dried fruit contains only fructose sugar, and you can buy pemmican and candy bars made with fructose at health-food and outdoor stores.

Most nutritionists think that carbohydrates should make up 50 to 60% of your regular diet. And some nutritionists say that a 70% carbohydrate intake is not too much when on a trip requiring high levels of exertion. Carbohydrates are the predominant food fuel during short-term, heavy exercise, and do much to maintain energy and prevent fatigue.

Protein

You may need to boost your carbohydrate intake when backpacking, but you don't need extra protein. Your protein intake should be about 12 to 15% of your diet.[1] Meat, fish, poultry, milk, nuts and eggs are good sources of protein. Since most foods containing complete proteins are heavy or tend to spoil easily, the best way for backpackers to get adequate protein is by combining several foods to get complementing proteins.

Backpackers going on long trips should have a working knowledge of complementary protein relationships. The basic rules for combining foods to get complete proteins are to eat legumes at the same meal as grains; legumes with nuts or seeds; and eggs or dairy products with any grains. This translates into some familiar food combinations we often eat together anyway: beans and rice; macaroni and cheese; cereal and milk; rice pudding; cornbread and lentil soup.

We get an extra bonus when we combine carbohydrates to make complete proteins, too—the combining foods count for our needs in both

---

1   The Department of Agriculture and Health and Human Services document *Nutrition and Your Health, Dietary Guidelines for Americans* 2nd ed., 1985

carbohydrate and protein categories. For more information on complementary proteins see Frances Moore Lappé's landmark book *Diet for a Small Planet.*

Gorging on a big thick steak the first night out may satisfy some ideas people have about pioneers braving the wilds, but it's not nutritionally sound. It's a huge amount of protein to consume all at once, and the steak is probably high in fat. Both fats and protein take much more water to digest than carbohydrates and we backpackers already need to drink lots and lots of water, especially at higher altitudes. Studies show that high protein diets appear to be the worst choice for cold weather, too. Compared with diets high in carbos or fats, high protein diets increase water requirements and reduce cold tolerance.[2]

Fats

Don't underestimate the importance of fats. While carbos give you quick energy, fats are your source of long-term energy. They'll help you to hike all day long, and keep you warm through the night. They're our most concentrated source of calories, too. Foods high in fat give us the most calories for the least weight, something hikers carrying food for a week or more need to consider. Also, since fats take about 4 hours to digest, they slow the emptying of the stomach and delay hunger. Your fat intake can range from 15 to 25% of your summer backpacking diet, and as high as 40% is OK in winter.

Cutting down on fat in the diet is a good idea most of the time, but if you greatly restrict your fat intake you may find that you get cold easily. "Sleeping cold" can often be remedied by adding butter or margarine to a cup of hot chocolate at bedtime and by eating more fats—cheese, margarine, butter, chocolate, oils, nuts, and nut butters.

2   "Nutrition for a Cold Environment," *The Physician and Sportsmedicine*, Vol. 17, No. 12 (December 1989): p. 77.

Calorie Division

There are a lot of theories floating around about the most favorable division of your caloric intake, but a reasonable guide for summer backpackers is 15 to 20% protein, 15 to 25% fats, and about 60 to 70% carbohydrates. You may want to take a multivitamin daily if you're going on a long trip, but don't worry about calculating grams of protein, fats, and carbos. Simply hit every food group each day: eat bread and grains, fruits and vegetables, a little protein, and some cheese or milk and you'll be fine.

Salt

Many people these days avoid salty foods, a good idea for our everyday lives, but when we've lost salt from sweating and due to the exertion of backpacking, it's wise to replenish it. Salt balance is essential to a feeling of well-being. Excessive fatigue, headache, and stomach cramps can be signs of salt deficiency. People who have eliminated salt from their everyday diets should lightly salt food at wilderness meals (do not take salt tablets). Many hikers find they crave salt and enjoy salty snacks they seldom eat at home such as salami and salted peanuts, especially when hiking in hot weather.

In the past few years people generally have developed healthier eating habits, but if taken to extremes some of the more popular eating trends—such as radically restricting fats, salt, and sugar from the diet—can be inadequate for people carrying a backpack. I remember a 29-year-old weightlifter on one trip. She was in excellent shape, but by the third day of our trip she was lagging behind the others and feeling ill. She had been eating mostly steamed potatoes, absolutely no fat and very little sugar. For lunch each day she'd limited herself to one "health bar." We finally convinced her that her low energy and bad mood were caused by her inadequate diet, and the next day, after eating two good meals she steamed down the trail with no more problems.

**Eat
Frequently**

We need to eat often while carrying a pack. This is not the time to fast or to diet. People who don't usually eat breakfast need to eat before starting down the trail in the morning, and you should snack between meals. While carrying a pack, nibble every couple of hours, more often than that if you're hungry. Keep snacks handy and eat plenty of carbos: leftover pasta and grains, trail mix, cookies, bread, crackers, dried fruit, or candy bars. Leftover breakfast is good trail food. Scoop what's left of the couscous or bulgur out of the breakfast pot, add honey or jam if you wish, put it in a ziploc bag and snack on it for the rest of the day.

Here's another trail food tip. Trail mix is actually an excellent backpacking food, but many people get sick of it if they eat it day after day. Time and again on longer trips I have seen people trying to give away their trail mix, but others seldom want it. Hence, you may want to alternate trail mix with a hearty, sweet bread. My favorite trail-snack breads are *Buckwheat Molasses Mountain Bread* (page 130), *Oat Date Bread* (page 129) and *Mers Prune Cake* (page 125).

Most backpackers have prodigious appetites, but for the first night of a backpacking trip, plan a lighter meal. The "backpacking metabolism" takes a day or two to kick in, and most people aren't as hungry on the first day or so of a trip—especially if the first night is spent at high elevation. Years ago I served a big spicy chicken dinner to my group for our first night's meal at altitude 11,000 feet. I'd cooked it ahead of time and served it in camp on a steaming bed of couscous with a sauce of raisins, pine nuts, spices and onions. People barely touched it. Since I wasn't at all hungry myself, I could hardly feel offended. After that I learned to serve soup and bread, cookies and herb tea on the first night.

**Dehydration,
Altitude and
Your
Appetite**

Whether you're backpacking at high altitudes or at sea level, in hot or cold weather, remember: *Drink lots of water.* Dehydration makes you more susceptible to hypothermia, frostbite, mountain sickness, and heat stroke.

The most common reason for feeling out-of-sorts on a backpacking trip is mild dehydration. I have seen this over and over. Usually if a person doesn't drink, it's because they don't feel thirsty. You can be dehydrated and not feel thirsty.

If you're backpacking in very hot weather, you'll need to drink 4 to 6 liters of water during a day on the trail. Don't drink sugar drinks on a hot day. When you're exercising in heat, sugar drinks retard movement of liquid out of the stomach, which may, in effect, promote dehydration. Four liters is probably enough for most people to consume when backpacking in typical mountain weather in the summer. In winter you'll need to drink at least 5 liters per day. Increase these amounts if you're at elevations above 8000 feet. The higher you go, the more liquids you'll need to consume.

If you're urinating several times a day and your urine is light yellow, you're probably drinking enough water; if your urine is dark yellow, drink more water. One sign of good acclimation to high altitude is increased frequency of urination, so that's a good check that you're acclimating.

Backpackers get thirsty at night; take a full water bottle to bed with you. I often see people refusing liquids around bedtime. They explain that they don't want to have to get up in the middle of the night. This is not smart at high elevation. The first night at elevations above 10,000 feet, I'll often get up three times during the night. Drink liquids even at bedtime, and when you have to get up in the night just think of it as a chance to contemplate the stars.

Most people experience some loss of appetite for awhile at elevations of 10,000 feet and higher. Foods you usually love don't taste good (although some other foods may become more appealing). If you don't feel like eating, drink soup. Keep hot water going in the cooking pot and pass around herb teas (chamomile is especially pleasing), packets of thin instant soups, hot chocolate, and instant apple juice.

At high elevations, most people prefer blander food and usually carbohydrates are more palatable than fats or proteins. This is another good reason why my spicy, high protein chicken dinner wasn't eaten at 11,000 feet. A low salt, high-carbohydrate diet is best up high. High elevation has a radical effect on cooking time, too. See page 84 for tips on cooking at altitude.

Alcohol is dehydrating and it also tends to have a stronger effect on people in the mountains, so go easy and don't overindulge. Caffeine is a diuretic, so coffee and tea consumption should be limited. High-altitude campers really go for sugars but, believe it or not, tend to pass up high-fat chocolates for hard-sugar candies like lemon drops and Kendal Mint Cake. This peppermint-and-sugar candy has no appeal for me except when I'm climbing at altitudes above 10,000 feet—and then it's wonderful. Kendal Mint Cake and lots of water have gotten many a climber to a mountaintop.

Most of us feel some of the symptoms of mountain sickness when we go to 10,000 feet and higher: lethargy, shortness of breath and higher pulse rate, fluid retention, sleeplessness, loss of appetite, headache and flu-like symptoms. These symptoms usually go away when we've acclimated, in about 24 to 48 hours. But it should be noted that high altitude can be life threatening for some people. In addition to the symptoms of ordinary mountain sickness, symptoms of HACE (high-altitude cerebral edema) include difficulty in walking and speaking, and symptoms of HAPE (high-altitude pulmonary edema) include cough and a gurgling sound in the lungs. The only treatment for both is immediate evacuation to a lower altitude.

Drinking copious amounts of liquids and eating carbohydrates helps us to adapt to high altitude, but the best way to mitigate the effects of high altitude is acclimation. If you're going high, spend the first night at the trailhead: sleep at about 6000 to 8000 feet before starting your hike.

Constipation

Constipation on the trail is a common problem, probably caused by the long drive to the trailhead, being off a regular routine, and lacking fiber in the diet. Being slightly dehydrated and hiking with a snug backpack belt around your middle don't help matters either. Here are some things you can do to prevent constipation. Eat lots of roughage a few days before and during your trip: prunes, pears, prune juice, bran muffins. Don't eat cheese, apples, or bananas—these foods tend to have the opposite effect. Do drink lots and lots of water. If stricken while on your trip, take two tablespoons of bran and/or a few prunes in the morning. Coffee helps, too. Metamucil, a natural-fiber laxative, comes in individual foil packets and is drunk mixed with water or juice. Consider a drug-type laxative only if you become uncomfortably constipated.

Good Food Makes for Good Spirits

We all know what it feels like to be hungry and short-tempered. Then we eat, and the world is a friendlier place. But sometimes someone on a trip gets into camp exhausted and wants to go to bed without any dinner. This is usually not a good idea. People should be encouraged to eat unless they are really ill, in which case party members must keep a close eye on them. Usually, bringing the disheartened hiker a cup of hot soup, communication, and friendly encouragement do wonders to revive a tired body and low spirits.

Hypothermia

Stories abound of hypothermia victims who had neglected to eat. Hypothermia, commonly known as "exposure," is the lowering of the body core temperature caused by exposure to cold and aggravated by water, wind, and exhaustion. People who are becoming hypothermic first shiver, then lose their judgment and reasoning power. They say things that don't make sense, slur their words, stumble, and do inappropriate things like taking off their clothes. They lag behind, urge others to go on without them, and deny they're in trouble. Since loss of judgment is one of the signs of hypothermia, it's important that people stick together and keep an eye on each other in hypothermic weather conditions.

Hypothermia can be prevented by dressing warmly, avoiding exhaustion and exposure, nibbling frequently, drinking hot liquids, not skipping meals, and not becoming dehydrated.

Whenever I hear of people running into this kind of trouble in the wilderness, my first question is "When did they last eat?" The story of two men who died of hypothermia on Mt. Rainier in 1989 is typical. The party of four drove until late at night to get there, dug a snow cave to sleep in, and after only a couple of hours of sleep started up the mountain without taking time to even boil water for hot drinks and cereal. Two lagged behind and two went on ahead. A storm hit and the two men ahead sought shelter in a crevasse. The other two, certainly hypothermic and losing their judgment, walked by the crevasse, continued climbing and died in the storm.

Several factors tipped the scales toward tragedy: lack of sleep, the party not sticking together, the storm, no hot food or drinks to fuel and warm tired bodies. Yet major happenings in life turn on small things. There's a good chance the deaths could have been prevented if time had been taken for hot drinks and food. Hot liquids and nourishment would have made them more alert, and possibly more aware of each other.

You may never find yourself in a situation where you're seeking shelter from a snowstorm in a crevasse, but there's a good lesson here. Even if you've had to set up camp in the rain and all you want to do is hunker down in your sleeping bag, you and your camping companions should make the effort to prepare a hot meal. If not a hot meal, then a cold meal—but eat something. Food brings people together and makes them feel better. The physical, psychological, and spiritual benefits of good food to a wilderness party can hardly be overestimated.

3

Menu Planning

In the last chapter you were encouraged to snack between meals and to indulge in hearty feasts, but now I must tell you that the most common mistake backpackers make is to bring too much food. I've heard stories of people running out of food in the wilderness, but the fact is that most people overburden their packs with more food than they can possibly eat.

It's true that most people eat more food when carrying a pack than at home, but keep in mind that you'll have to pack out whatever you don't eat. This chapter gives you practical guidelines for planning the right amounts of food for your backpacking trip and for creating a menu that works well with your trip plan. Your personal style must be considered when planning menus, too, and *Chapter 4* has four menus designed for specific trips and individual styles—from gourmet campers to Spartan peakbaggers.

Carefully planning your menu is critical. Start by making a menu chart. It should list the days of your trip, the miles you plan to hike each day, the elevations of your camps, and the number of people in your party. Your menu chart will guide you in planning meals that suit your trip plan and in figuring amounts. You should work from it when packing food, and carry it with you on the trail.

Tailoring Your Menu To Your Trip Plan

There's no set rule as to how much each day's food should weigh—it's the length of your trip that determines the weight of your food. You can carry heavier fresh food for a weekend trip, but on longer trips you have to bring nonperishable and lightweight foods. You can use some fresh food for the first few days of a long trip, and plan menus around the perishability of food. (See *Chapter 5* for tips on packing and extending the life of fresh foods.) A party of four going out for a week or more should certainly be able to keep food weight to 2½ pounds of food per person per day. Using dried and calorie-concentrated foods, it's possible to keep weight to a low 1½ pounds per person per day.

On days where many miles are to be covered, plan big breakfasts and lots of lunch food to fuel hard-working bodies. Evening meals should be hearty, but easy to prepare. You won't want to cook an elaborate meal after a 12-mile day on the trail, but on a rest day it might be fun to serve a fancy dinner.

It will save time to cook extra food sometimes so there will be leftovers to eat for the next meal. Leftover lentil soup for breakfast can help you get an early start, and extra pasta from dinner becomes a pasta salad for lunch.

The elevation of your camp is always an important consideration in menu planning. Food takes longer to cook at high elevation, and most pastas turn to wallpaper paste above 10,000 feet, so don't plan a spaghetti dinner for the nights you'll camp at high altitudes. Remember that most people aren't very hungry at high altitudes or on the first night of a trip. Also remember to bring herb teas, soups and drinks to tempt people to consume lots of liquids at high elevation.

People are usually extra tired the first night out. We *ought* to get to bed early the night before leaving on a trip, but most of us seldom do. It's therefore a good idea to plan a quick and easy meal for the first night. If you cook a one-pot meal ahead of time and freeze it so all you have to do is warm it up in camp, you'll be glad you did.

Don't think that the one-pot meal is *de rigueur* for cooking on the one-burner backpacking stove, but don't get carried away with multicourse meals if you don't have some experience cooking on a backpacking stove. Although you may enjoy spending a couple of hours preparing a great meal in your home kitchen, you may not feel the same way after a day of schlepping a pack up a mountain trail. Also, stay away from foods that take a long time to cook. For example, regular brown rice, which takes 45 minutes to cook at sea level, is an impractical backpacking food.

Consider the weather when planning your menu, and always carry a small amount of "bail-out" food with you. Extra instant soups, bouillon cubes, and freeze-dried dinners can be life savers if you get caught in bad weather or arrive in camp late and tired.

Factor the time of year into your plans, too. For example, for a hike in California in June you'll have light until 8 or 9 o'clock, probably plenty of time to set up camp and prepare a 3-course meal; in October you'll want to have dinner over with and the dishes done by nightfall at around 6 PM.

A winter trip allows you to bring foods that need to be refrigerated, but you need to consume more calories, too. Since fats help keep you warm and high-fat foods are also concentrated calories, foods that are higher in fat are just right for winter trips.

Am I going to bear country? This is something I always consider when planning my menu. Why have a luscious piece of bacon hanging in the food bag? You might not be able to smell it, but its fragrance will make Mr. Bear's mouth water and possibly cause him to hang around all night trying to get at your food.

Is water available? On our yearly trip to the Grand Canyon we have a dry camp one night on the Tonto Plateau. Since we start the day carrying 4 to 6 liters of water (8 to 12 pounds) we carry lightweight food, and we don't take foods like pasta that require cooking with lots of water.

Figuring Amounts

How much food can a hungry backpacker eat? There's no need to get hung up on figuring calories—but if you want numbers, here's a rough guide. Backpackers usually consume 3200 to 4200 calories a day. When carrying a 40-pound pack, a 120 pound person burns 340 calories an hour while a 180 pound person burns 472 calories per hour.[1]

People usually eat 10 to 20% more on easy backpacking trips, 30% more on moderate trips, and 50 to 100% as much on very strenuous trips. The amount of food people eat depends on age, sex, weight, individual metabolism, and other things. Men usually eat about a third more than women, and teenagers eat about 1½ times as much as adults.

You'll be most correct in figuring amounts if you know about the eating habits of your group. Find out about the likes, dislikes, and food allergies of group members. Whatever you do, be certain to ask how many cups of coffee people drink in the morning. Backcountry cooks can get away with burning dinner or serving spicy-hot dishes to people who would rather be eating oatmeal—but running out of coffee is an unforgivable crime!

After you make your overall meal plan and learn something about the eating habits of your group, you can get down to figuring amounts. Guessing

---

1   C.B. Corbin and R. Lindsey, *Fitness for Life*, 2nd ed. (Glenview, IL: Scott, Foresman and Co., 1983), p. 105.

will get you by on short trips with few people, but for long trips or larger groups you must be more exact. To calculate amounts accurately, work from your menu chart meal-by-meal. Make a list of the foods and the amounts needed for each meal, then add up the amounts you need of each food. An amounts-needed list of some items for a large group might look something like this:

Dry milk: 1½, ½, ½, 1, ½ = 4 cups
Oil: 5 TB, 4 TB, ½ cup, ¼ cup, 2 TB, 1 TB, 1 TB = 1½ cups
Coffee (fresh ground): ¾, ¾, ¾, 1½, 1½, = 5¼ cups (about 13 ounces)
Hot chocolate: 8, 8, 8, 8, = 32 packages
Miso soup: 8, 8, = 16 packages
Garlic cloves: 1, 4, 2, 4 = 11 cloves

People often have a hard time estimating amounts of pasta, rice and other carbohydrates. Estimating how much each person will eat depends on what type of carbohydrate it is and what else you're eating for that meal. Bulgur seems to be the most filling grain. Regular white rice is more satisfying than Minute Rice. For Minute Rice, I usually figure on ½ to ¾ cup of uncooked rice per person. About ⅓ cup of uncooked bulgur, quick brown rice, regular white rice and most other grains equal one serving for a hungry backpacker. Two ounces of pasta is about right for one small serving for a woman; for a dinner with pasta as the main course, 6 ounces of pasta should be enough for a hungry backpacking man and woman. You can use suggested serving amounts on food boxes as a guide—but increase the amounts by about one-third for one serving.

As you can see, there's always some guesswork involved. But beware of bringing too much food, especially for longer trips. The longer your trip, the more precise you have to be. Estimate as closely as you can, add any second helpings judiciously, and refrain from throwing in "one for the pot" for every meal.

Keep records of how much food you take with you and how much you have to carry home. Know how much of your brand of coffee you consumed per day, make notes of foods you got tired of, and of foods you craved. Records from your last trip will make getting ready for your next trip much easier.

When you're finally ready to load up your backpack and start down the trail, I suggest that you lay out all the food on a surface and take a good look at it. This is an especially good practice if you've divided up the menu so different people are responsible for different meals. Lay out your food meal by meal and in daily order: breakfasts across the top of the tarp, lunches in the middle, dinners along the bottom. This gives you a chance to actually see all the food instead of thinking about it in terms of individual meals—and to eliminate what you can.

The Final Touch

You may come out of the wilderness with a powerful craving for a hamburger or a big salad, but the first thing most people want is an ice-cold beer!

So if you want to give everyone a fine treat at the end of the trail, surprise them with cold beer and juice you've left in the camp cooler back at the car. A cooler left in the trunk of your car insulated with an old sleeping bag or blanket and containing three large blocks of ice should keep a six-pack and a few cans of pineapple juice good and cold for about five days.

4

Menus Tailored to Your Trip and Your Style

Are you looking for a menu of easy-to-prepare food? Maybe you want a gourmet menu for a romantic weekend in the mountains. Are you getting ready for your trip at the last minute? Perhaps you're planning a lightweight, high-energy menu for a 10-day trek, or will be cooking meals at high elevation for a week. This chapter features four sample menus, and gives you tips for tailoring your menus to specific trips and to your individual style.

The *Fast Food* section below shows you several ways you can minimize cooking time on the trail and includes advice for people who don't care for cooking but want healthful food, good taste, and variety in their wilderness diet. The *Peakbaggers Fast Food Weekend Menu* is appropriate for high altitude cooking, and all meals on it can be prepared in 15 minutes or less.

The next menu—*Romantic Gourmets*—is for serious hedonists. This section tells you how to make your trail meals a dining experience. There are tips on how to create just the right romantic atmosphere, with a menu that features flaming desserts, fine wines, and expensive imported food.

Following *Romantic Gourmets* is the menu I use for my groups on Call of the Wild's annual backpack to the summit of Mt. Whitney. This 6-day menu has been planned for a group of eight or more and uses mostly fresh food, but there are ways of making changes in the menu that would lighten the load considerably if you have just two or three people. Finally, there's the *Ten-Day Trekkers Menu* focusing on light weight and relying on grains and home-dried food.

All menus have been planned with good nutrition and taste in mind. The meals are intended to offer variety, and they often include a side dish or two. If you want to simplify your own menu, you can eliminate these side dishes and have just the main course. Recipes for every dish on these menus can be found in the recipe section and are shown in italics.

Fast Food

If you don't want to spend much time cooking at home or on the trail, your local deli, gourmet shop or health-food store is your best source for quick meals. You can easily provision a weekend trip of quick-and-easy meals on your way out of town with one stop at a grocery store that has a delicatessen. For more information refer to *Chapter 1, The Backpacker's Groceries*.

Using freeze-dried food or other kinds of prepackaged meals saves both pre-trip and in-camp preparation time. Although it is expensive, you may find it worthwhile to use this kind of food for a few of your meals—but if so be prepared to sacrifice taste for convenience.

Cooking most of your food at home is the best way to minimize cooking time on the trail. Just about any one-pot meal can be prepared in advance, put in a sealable plastic bag and frozen, then thawed and heated for dinner the first or second night out.

Spaghetti, curry, or a pot of beans make a simple and satisfying camp meal and taste even better when flavors have been given a chance to marry. Most of the recipe chapters contain dishes you prepare at home and eat on the trail. See *Chapter 5, Packing Food and Keeping It Fresh* for packaging and safe care of fresh, precooked foods.

If you have the time and the inclination, making your own home-dried food is a satisfying and inexpensive way to create the makings of your own delicious, quick-and-easy meals for the trail; see *Chapter 8, Home-Drying Food*. You can also substitute freeze-dried vegetables and fruit for home-dried food in any recipe in this book.

Make quick-cooking grains the backbone of your wilderness diet. Use bulgur wheat, quick brown rice, and instant couscous. Angel hair (also called **capellini**) is the fastest-cooking dry pasta. For a special treat try fresh pasta from the deli—it cooks in about 5 minutes. A simple baked potato is satisfying and can be baked ahead of time and simply reheated on the trail.

I think Top Ramen, Minute Rice, and instant mashed potatoes (brands without salt and other additives) are good choices for backpackers who don't want to fuss with cooking—if you boost the flavor and the nutritional value of these fast foods. This can be done by adding seeds, nuts, and even wheat germ, and they can be dressed up instantly with extras, too. Flake smoked salmon, canned chicken, or good old tunafish onto Minute Rice; stir imported Parmesan cheese and real butter into instant mashed potatoes; drop a spoonful of pesto from the deli into Ramen.

The secret is to use high-quality ingredients whenever possible. People who don't care much about cooking often think that the quality of ingredients used in a dish doesn't matter, but using high-quality ingredients improves both taste and nutrition.

The following 3-day menu requires minimal at-home and in-camp preparation. Boiling water for Minute Rice, pasta, and couscous is the only cooking required, so your meals can be ready in less than 15 minutes from the time you start your stove. If you're at high elevation when you have the pasta dinner, use either Ramen or fresh pasta. The ingredients shown in italics are found in the Recipes chapters.

Peakbaggers Fast Food Weekend Menu

Fri. lunch   Whole wheat bread
Monterey Jack cheese
Celery, carrot
Raisins and sunflower seeds

Fri. dinner   Instant Minestrone soup mix
Basil Pesto with pasta
Wheat bread, butter
Cookies
Hot chocolate, herb teas

Sat. breakfast   *Summit Breakfast* (couscous with dates) or
packaged instant cereal fortified with seeds, wheatgerm, or nuts
Tang
Coffee, tea
English muffins (toasted or plain), butter and jam

Sat. lunch   Leftover pasta and *pesto* (now it's pasta salad)
Whole wheat bread, butter
Celery, carrot
Oatmeal cookies
Dried apricots
Kendal Mint Cake

Sat. dinner   Instant Miso soup mix
Szechuan Snow Peas over Minute Rice
Fortune cookies
Dried pineapple
Hot chocolate

Sun. breakfast   Granola with dry milk and dried fruit
English muffins, butter and jam
Coffee, tea
Tang

Sun. lunch   Smoked cheese
Whole wheat bread
Apple
Fig Newtons
Trail mix

Romantic Gourmets

In spite of a reputation for Spartanlike leanings, many backpackers are actually hedonists at heart. These hikers believe that fine food is good for the soul, and they understand the subtle yet important role champagne and caviar can play in furthering a romance. For these people I've planned a special menu for a long weekend. But before we get into the food, here are some tips for creating just the right atmosphere.

If you're celebrating a birthday, you may want to make it a surprise party like one of my friends did. Before leaving home she baked a tiny cake in a shortbread cookie tin and quietly tucked away some party favors in her pack. On the big day, her boyfriend went fishing. When he returned to camp her dogs ran out to greet him wearing party hats. Crepe paper streamers festooned the trees and balloons were everywhere, and there were candles on the cake.

Maybe you'd prefer a more romantic, Omar Khayyam-type ambiance. To get that "loaf of bread, jug of wine, and thou beside me singing in the wilderness" effect, serve dinner to your beloved on a white paper tablecloth with candles (or a candle lantern), a bouquet of wildflowers (where permissible), a couple of bandanas for napkins and, of course, a nalgene bottle of wine. Plastic wine glasses with screw-on stems are fine. I know one extravagant soul who packed in a bottle of 1967 Châteauneuf du Pape, crystal goblets, and silverware, but unless you're planning to propose this is probably going too far.

The following menu for a three-day trip would be most appropriate for an itinerary with low daily mileage. Better yet, make a base camp and just stay put. To allow yourself maximum time for romance in the wilderness, most of the cooking should be done ahead of time.

Romantic Gourmets Lost Weekend Menu

Fri. lunch   Goat cheese
             Herbed Sun-Dried Tomatoes In Olive Oil
             Calamata olives
             Baguette
             Nectarines
             Italian macaroons

Fri. dinner *Marrakech Soup*
             Spring Lamb Curry and Couscous
             Condiments: chutney, minced green onions,
                coconut, raisins, peanuts, banana
             Pita bread
             Cucumbers with yogurt and dill
             Zinfandel
             Halvah
             Mint tea

Sat. breakfast Scrambled eggs with salsa
             Hash Brown Sweet Potatoes with Cilantro Pesto
             Corn tortillas
             Coffee, tea

Sat. lunch   Smoked oysters
             Aged Gouda cheese
             Jono's Herb Rolls
             Apple
             Biscotti

Sat. dinner Proscuitto-wrapped cantaloupe slices
             Puttanesca with Goat Cheese and Angel Hair Pasta
             Blood Oranges and Capers with Spring-Mix
                Baby Lettuces
             Dijon-Balsamic Vinaigrette
             Baguette
             Barbera (or some other red wine served at
                mountain air temperature)
             Cherries Jubilee
             Ginseng tea

Sun. breakfast *Buckwheat Cakes*
             Strawberry Sauce
             Pancetta
             Coffee
             More ginseng tea

Sun. lunch   Pâté
             Fancy mustards—2 or 3 kinds in film containers
             Cornichons
             Rye bread
             Kiwi fruit

Back at the car you've left a bottle of champagne on a block of ice in a camp cooler for the end-of-the-trail celebration. Serve with caviar, then head for the nearest hot springs.

Group Menu

Now we're getting serious. This is the menu I use for my yearly 6-day backpacking trip to the summit of Mt. Whitney. Most of our meals are cooked at elevations above 11,000 feet; we hike a total of 42 miles, daily mileage ranges from 5 to 13 miles; there's one rest day.

Since this menu is designed for a group, we can afford to have more luxuries and fresh foods because the weight of the group equipment is distributed among more people. If you have only two or three people, you can still use this basic menu, but you might want to cut out some heavier items. You can, for example, substitute cookies or eliminate some of the heavier dessert breads. Instead of fresh eggs and fresh cabbage, substitute dehydrated eggs and home-dried cabbage. Make the dehydrated curried lentil soup on page 169 instead of *Dahl Shorba* (page 149).

Remember that figuring the right amounts becomes even more important on longer trips. On a short trip, you can bring some extra food "just to make sure," but if you do this on a longer trip you will overburden your back.

Mt. Whitney 6-Day Menu

Sun. Lunch *Cottonwood Pass (11,200')*
Pre-baked potatoes
Bread and cheese
Apple
Carrot

Sun. Dinner *Chicken Spring Lake (11,200')*
People usually aren't hungry this day because it's the first day of the trip and because of the effect of high elevation on appetite.
Whole wheat bread
Thai Tom Yum soup
Madeline's Jam Squares
Lemon Zinger or chamomile tea

Mon. Breakfast	***Chicken Spring Lake (11,200')***
	Green onion zucchini omelette
	Whole wheat toast, butter and jam
	Coffee, tea
Mon. Lunch	***On the trail***
	Smoked tofu
	Cheese
	Dijon mustard
	Crackers
	Madeline's Jam Squares
	Trail mix
Mon. Dinner	***Rock Creek (9500')***
	Basil Pesto with Angel hair pasta
	Salad: iceberg lettuce, red onion, rice vinegar
	dressing
	Lemon Loaf Cake
	Hot chocolate
Tues. Breakfast	***Rock Creek (9500')***
	Home-dried hash browns
	Whole wheat English muffins, jam
	Coffee, tea
Tues. Lunch	***Rock Creek (9500')***
	Leftovers: Pasta salad and hash browns
	Dry jack cheese
	Whole wheat English muffins
	Dried fruit
Tues. Dinner	***Rock Creek (9500')***
	Buttermilk Cornbread
	Dahl Shorba (curried lentil soup)
	Chutney
	Mint tea
	Kiwi fruit slices
Wed. Breakfast	***Rock Creek (9500')***
	House of the Sun Bulgur
	Coffee, tea
Wed. Lunch	***On the trail***
	Leftover *Bulgur*
	Hummus
	Crackers
	High-Power Peanut Butter
	Pilot bread (or some other hard, dense cracker)
	Apple
Wed. Night	***Guitar Lake (11,500')***
	Instant Miso soup
	12,000' Oriental Stir-Fry
	Minute Rice
	Herb teas

Fortune cookies

Thurs. Breakfast   **Guitar Lake (11,500')**
Summit Breakfast
Coffee, tea

Thurs. Lunch   **Mt. Whitney Summit**
Leftover couscous
Cheese, Dijon mustard
Crackers
Kendal Mint Cake
PowerBar, dried fruit

Thurs. Dinner   **Trail Camp (12,000')**
Mexican Chicken Tostadas with cabbage, dry jack
cheese, avocados, salsa, onion, refried beans
(Fantastic Foods or home-dried)
Minute Rice
Hot chocolate, herb teas

Fri. Breakfast   **Trail Camp (12,000')**
Instant Cream of Wheat
Dry milk
Coffee, tea

Fri. Lunch   **On the trail**
High-Power Peanut Butter
Crackers
Dried fruit

Trekkers Menu

On a 10-day trip the weight of your food becomes even more important, and most backpackers feel that about 10 days worth of food is close to the limit they want to carry. Hikers will usually arrange a food drop every 10 days or exit and resupply.

This 10-day menu relies on grains, foods with concentrated calories such as nut butter spreads, and home-dried food. Most people going on long treks have no-frills food, but you can have more variety and tastier food by provisioning your long trip with home-dried food. *Chapter 8* tells you how to dry your own backpacking food at home.

As you should expect for a 10-day trip, this menu takes many hours of pretrip preparation, but since most meals are made from home-dried food there's a minimum of cooking to do on the trail. The baked goods are the only foods that require much preparation time in camp, but the taste of fresh-baked bread after days on the trail will convince you it's time well spent. You can substitute store-bought baked goods if you wish.

If you want to simplify this menu—spending less time with pretrip preparation—rotate the same meals every few days. I once met a Canadian hiking the Pacific Crest Trail who was rotating the same three dinners day after blessed day for his 3-month trip. This would bore me to death, but he was cheerfully covering around 20 miles a day.

Cooking some extra dinner and breakfast to eat at lunch can simplify your menu and help shave a bit of weight from your pack, too. Since usual lunch food is heavy, preparing extra dinner servings and making more pancakes and cereal at breakfast will trim some weight from your pack. The only drawback is that you must have the willpower to save the extra food for lunch.

Good food plays an important role in helping you to keep a positive attitude on a long trip. People who have been on long hiking trips know that food can make or break a trip. If you want to simplify, go ahead and repeat a few meals in this menu, but remember that you need some variety to keep you happily looking forward to dinner.

Ten-Day Trekkers Menu
Day 1
Breakfast	*Scottish Prunes*	
	English muffins	
	Coffee, tea	
Lunch	Smoked tofu	
	Celery, carrots	
	Rye bread	
	Trail mix	
Dinner	*South of the Border Pesto* with corn ribbons (or other pasta)	
	Iceberg lettuce salad with rice vinegar dressing	

Day 2
Breakfast	Freeze-dried omelette
	English muffins
Lunch	Rye bread

Baked potatoes with leftover *pesto*
Mer's Prune Cake

Dinner *Good Old Macaroni and Cheese*
Nightcap Apricots

Day 3

Breakfast *House of the Sun Bulgur*
Coffee, tea

Lunch Hummus
Celery
Honey-Date Cashew Butter
Mer's Prune Cake

Dinner Instant Miso soup mix
Szechuan Snow Peas over Minute Rice
Almond cookies
Jasmine tea

Day 4

Breakfast *Buckwheat Cakes* with maple syrup
Coffee, tea

Lunch Smoked Gouda
Leftover *Buckwheat Cakes*
Cookies
Trail mix

Dinner *Leek and Potato Soup*
Sunflower-Caraway Cabbage Salad (home-dried)
Chocolate-Almond Brownies

Day 5

Breakfast Granola
Dry milk
Coffee, tea

Lunch *Honey-Date Cashew Butter*
Smoked Gouda
Pilot bread (or some other hard, dense cracker)
Apple
Mer's Prune Cake

Dinner *Near-East Far-Out Bulgur Chicken*
Spicy Cumin Carrots
Mint tea

Day 6

Breakfast Whole wheat couscous with raisins and walnuts
Dry milk
Coffee, tea

Lunch Dry jack cheese
Leftover *Bulgur Chicken*
Crackers (hard crackers such as Wasa or Rye-Crisp)
Dates

Dinner	*Indian Sambaar Stew*
	Buttermilk Cornbread and butter
	Halvah
	Mint Tea

Day 7

Breakfast	Leftover *Buttermilk Cornbread* with maple syrup
	Coffee, tea
Lunch	*Honey-Date Cashew Butter*
	Crackers
	Orange
Dinner	*Sherried Mushrooms and Sweet Peppers* with rice
	Hazelnut Chocolate Mousse
	Hot chocolate

Day 8

Breakfast	*House of the Sun Bulgur*
	Coffee, tea
Lunch	Hummus
	Orange Marmalade-Almond Butter
	Crackers
	Dried fruit
Dinner	*Cream of Dilled Salmon*
	Minute Rice
	Mint tea, hot chocolate

Day 9

Breakfast	*Whole Wheat Pancakes*
	Coffee, tea
Lunch	*Orange Marmalade-Almond Butter*
	Dry jack cheese
	Crackers
	Apple
	Dried fruit
Dinner	*Black Bean Polenta Pie*
	Pear Torte

Day 10

Breakfast	Fried leftover *polenta*
	Maple syrup
	Coffee, tea
Lunch	*Orange Marmalade-Almond Butter*
	Dry jack cheese
	Crackers
	Trail mix
Dinner	Vegetarian burger mix with cheese
	Carrot-Raisin Salad (home-dried)
	Halvah
	Hot chocolate

5

Packing Food
and Keeping It Fresh

Packing food for your backpacking trip should not be put off till the last minute—that's my first bit of advice on this subject. Since I have spent more all-nighters prepping for trips than I care to remember, I know whereof I speak. There are a million things to do before a trip, and what you thought was an afternoon's work can continue on deep into the night.

The second bit of advice goes with the first: take the time to do as much preparation at home as possible. Your goals are to make meals easier to prepare in camp, to pack foods so they will stay fresh longer, and to make your load as light and as compact as you can. This is accomplished by repackaging, carefully measuring, and clearly labeling. Label everything, and include cooking directions on the label. Prewritten directions will help you stay organized and allow you to delegate cooking jobs, and a well-organized packing job will spare you the frustration of continually searching for things in camp.

Because the way you pack your food is basic to extending the life of perishables, this chapter not only tells you how to pack food at home to prolong freshness, but also gives you tips for keeping food fresh in the backcountry.

A Packing System

Devise a packing system to suit your style. Some people bag staples together: all the granola for the trip goes in one bag, all the bulgur in another. A spice bag is carried separately, all cheese is together, and so on. This system takes the least pre-trip preparation and is the most flexible. The major disadvantage is that meals in camp may take longer to prepare. Also, if you don't measure carefully when cooking in camp, you may run out of some ingredients before the trip's end.

Many people like to pack all food needed for one meal (or one day) together, down to the last detail. This method is not as flexible, and it requires the longest pre-trip prep. But it has major advantages: meals on the trail are quickly prepared, and since every ingredient is measured out per meal in advance, you're not likely to run out of anything.

Most of us use some combination of these two methods. Here's the packing system that works for me: I have a main supply of frequently used staples bagged in ziplocs: tea bags, coffee, sugar cubes, oil, butter, dry milk, jams, spices.

I make meal kits for breakfasts and dinners for each day. The meal kits are individually packaged in large ziploc bags and labeled, for example, "Wednesday Breakfast" or "Saturday Dinner."

A breakfast meal kit might contain a pancake mix that I've put together at home and labeled "Buckwheat Cakes. Add 1 cup H_2O." The breakfast kit would also contain a plastic bag of dried strawberries with a packet of cornstarch and sugar included inside. The label would say "Strawberry Sauce. Heat sugar/cornstarch with 1 cup H_2O in frying pan, stir constantly till thick then gently stir in rehydrated strawberries & heat through." The other breakfast foods—coffee, tea, butter, and so on would come from the staples bags.

People carry all their own lunches for the entire trip. This insures that no one is on the trail without ready-to-eat food.

It's wise to label all food in the meal kit with a designation for a particular meal. For example, a can of crab would have a label saying "Saturday Dinner." This makes things much easier when you need dinner ingredients, especially with groups of four or more. This is because food is redistributed every couple of days and gets moved from pack to pack because it's not fair for one person to carry an entire meal planned for the end of the trip day after day when everyone else's pack is getting lighter. Just make sure that slow hikers aren't carrying the stove, essential cooking pots, or that night's dinner.

For more meal kit examples, see the one-day menu at the end of this chapter, where you're taken through packing details step-by-step.

Repackaging Groceries

Repackaging means you'll carry less weight and bulk in your pack and have less garbage to carry home. Get rid of all extra packaging. Don't use glass containers; they're heavy, breakable, and completely impractical. Be aware that foil does not burn and must be packed out. Transfer food to bags and containers that are smaller, unbreakable, and leakproof. Here are the supplies you'll need for packaging your backpacking food:

Measuring cups and spoons
Ziploc bags, quart and gallon size (regular and freezer-weight)
Brown paper bags for packing fresh fruits and vegetables
Nalgene plastic bottles in a variety of sizes
Plastic food tubes
Self-adhesive labels
A ballpoint or indelible ink pen

Useful but not necessary is a food scale for weighing anything from an ounce to 10 pounds; the one I use costs under $15.

Another thing which almost seems to have been designed for backpackers is the Seal-A-Meal. This little machine costs about $20 and self-seals tough, boilable plastic bags into any size or shape you need—from a tiny spice packet to a large bag of bulgur.

A more expensive alternative to the Seal-A-Meal are home vacuum-packaging machines. They cost from $50 to $300. I use the FoodSaver brand of this machine, and it's wonderful. Vacuum packaging is a great way to keep home-dried foods fresh longer, and you can use vacuum packaging for grains, your own soup mixes, and so on. Don't vacuum-package food that needs refrigeration unless you keep it refrigerated. This is because with certain foods harmful bacteria can grow in low-oxygen environments at temperatures from 40 to 115 degrees. You don't have to use the vacuum feature with the vacuum-packaging machine, however; you can use only the self-sealing feature if you wish.

Ziploc bags are best for bagging teas, trail mix, and other foods that you need to open many times. Both Seal-A-Meal and the FoodSaver machines make a nonleak permanant seal and are best used for packaging items you'll open only once. This fancy equipment is nice to have, but certainly not necessary. You can do just fine with a couple of boxes of ziplocs.

To begin repackaging, assemble your groceries and put your menu someplace where you can refer to it constantly. I tape mine on the refrigerator. To help yourself stay organized, set out three cardboard boxes (orange or apple boxes with lids are perfect) and label them "breakfasts," "lunches," and "dinners." As each item is repackaged, toss it into the appropriate box. You can transport food to the trailhead in these boxes, too. Perishable foods are kept in the refrigerator until departure time, then they get transferred to the camp cooler for transport to the trailhead.

I usually start by making a kitchen bag. Depending on your style and the size of your group you could include part or all of the following items in a ziploc bag: a small presoaped scrubber (the type that is sponge on one side, abrasive on the other); 2 or 3 ounces of dishwashing soap; matches; 3 or 4 folded squares of heavy-duty aluminum foil; a few folded squares of paper towels; a hot pad; a bandana and/or dishtowel; a couple of 13-gallon white plastic garbage bags; a large heavy-duty garbage bag.

Most of your repackaged food will go into plastic bags—ziploc bags are indispensible. I use freezer-weight ziploc bags for carrying teabags, hot chocolate and for other packages that will get a lot of use, medium-weight bags for most other things. Sometimes bags get punctured, so it's best to double-bag everything. The extra bags can be used later for carrying leftovers for lunch. To prevent plastic bags from blowing up like balloons when you travel to a high altitude, press air out of them before sealing at home.

Boxed dry food is best repackaged into plastic bags. Sometimes there's a temptation to throw an entire box into your pack even though there's at least a cup too much, but remember that every little bit of extra weight counts. It's usually worth it to repackage. If you include the recipe from the cardboard box in your plastic bag, make sure to cut it out with rounded corners so sharp corners won't poke a hole in the plastic.

Mixes for pancakes, cornbread, and cobbler go into plastic bags and should be double-bagged. Sometime labels fall off, so always affix labels to plastic bags containing the food, then slip the second bag over the labeled bag. It's easier to put the label on the bag before you add the food.

Be sure to write out complete directions; you may not remember all the details of the recipe several days down the trail. The label for apple cobbler might read "Apple Cobbler. Mix spice packet with dry apples, then rehydrate in 2 cups hot H_20 in 3-qt pot. Add 1 cup cold H_20 to flour in its bag. Mix together, then spoon over apple mixture. Simmer covered for at least 20 min."

Plastic food tubes can be filled and sealed from the bottom. They're good for transporting nut butters, mustard, honey, and jellies. Enclose them in quart-size ziplocs to avoid leakage.

Be careful about using just any plastic container for repackaging liquids. Most of them leak. The nalgene bottles sold at your outdoor store are wonderful for carrying liquids because they don't leak as long as you give the lid an extra twist, and they are the safest way I know to carry oils, which are especially apt to leak. Be sure to give the lid an extra twist, then enclose the bottle in a ziploc bag just to make sure.

It's practical to carry all the oil you'll need for your trip in one container—but on longer trips this makes it easy to use too much at first and run out of oil the last few days. To guard against this, I mark levels on my cooking oil bottle with a couple of pieces of freezer tape. At the highest level the tape is labeled, for example, "Wed. oil check," the next tape level might say "Sun. oil check."

Labels can help you ration other things, too. On a nalgene jam jar you might say "Raspberry jam. For Wed. and Thurs. lunch and Sun. pancakes" in hopes that this could possibly save it from being devoured too soon by hungry campers.

Nalgene bottles come in all sizes with both wide and narrow mouths. In the very large wide-mouth sizes, you can pack cookies, pasta, and other crushables. Your camp cooking pots are ideal for carrying crushables, too—breads, crackers, vegetables like cherry tomatoes.

Spices and condiments can go in the smallest nalgene bottles, although I prefer carrying spices in clear plastic film cans, all in one spice bag. Film cannisters are great for carrying lunch condiments, too—Dijon and Cajun mustard, and Thai chili paste. Wooden matches go in a very small wide-mouth nalgene bottle—it's just the right size and moisture can't get in. Tabasco sauce, soy sauce, dish soap, and iodine for purifying water go into little nalgene bottles with pop-up spouts.

The best way to carry butter or margarine is in wide-mouth nalgene containers. Plastic food tubes are a good way to carry butter, too, if you put the tube in a ziploc bag to ensure that it won't leak. Don't worry about butter spoiling. I have carried butter without refrigeration for up to a week in warm weather in the Grand Canyon and Hawaii. Carry regular salted butter and take care of it; don't let it melt or sit out in the sun.

Many people carry fresh eggs in the noncrushable plastic egg containers sold at outdoor stores, or you can carry eggs in the cardboard carton they're sold in. They will stay fresh without refrigeration for a week at least. To avoid having eggshells added to the garbage, you can break fresh eggs into a nalgene bottle at home. They spoil quickly, though, so unless you can keep them cold in a stream eat them for your first breakfast on the trail.

Whether you're filling bottles or food tubes, *never* fill them all the way to the top. If you do, they'll probably leak—especially if you're going to a higher elevation. And this point is worth repeating a second time: to prevent leakage, give the lids on nalgene bottles an extra twist.

Packaging Precooked Food

Meals you've cooked ahead for the first night's meal can be put in ziploc or Seal-A-Meal plastic bags and then refrigerated or frozen. Always double- or triple-bag to make sure they don't leak in your pack. This is where the strong, nonleak self-sealing plastic bags really come in handy. If you're feeding several people, it's better to split the meal into two bags rather than make one big unwieldy package. There's less chance of its getting punctured, and it will be easier to pack. Before leaving, put this food in your camp cooler for the trip to the trailhead. (Tip: It's easy to forget about food in the refrigerator or the freezer. Put a note on the front door or the steering wheel of your car so you'll remember to put that food into the cooler before driving off.)

Spoilage of precooked food won't be a problem if you take proper care. Don't let food sit out in the sun. To keep it cool for many hours, insulate it with layers of crumpled newspapers and carry it well protected from the sun in the middle of your pack. Don't expect to carry poultry and dishes containing cream, eggs, and other dairy products very long without refrigeration.

Some people eat pre-prepared dishes (but not poultry) the second night out. They start out with the meal frozen hard and well insulated in crumpled newspapers. This is not a smart thing to do in hot desert temperatures, but in normal summer temperatures in the mountains your food will stay cold. In fact, if you start hiking with your first night's dinner a frozen block, you will probably have to wait for it to thaw before you can eat.

Keeping Produce And Other Perishables Fresh

With proper care and packaging, fresh fruits and vegetables will keep a surprisingly long time. It's a simple formula: Don't cut them, don't wash them, and—above all—don't pack them in plastic bags. At the store choose vegetables that are fresh, unbruised, and unblemished. Most fresh vegetables will keep pretty well without refrigeration if they can breathe, so package them in brown paper lunch bags without crowding, and handle with care. Protect the more crushable veggies by carrying them in a cooking pot. To extend the life and freshness of veggies—or any foods—keep them cool and in the dark. Nothing will ruin food faster than sunlight.

Meats like salty ham, pancetta, proscuitto, and dry sausages such as Andouille, chorizo, linguisa, pepperoni, and summer sausages can be kept for several days, too. Just don't pack them in plastic.

Some fruits and vegetables that work well for backpacking are avocados, cabbages, carrots, celery, apples, kiwi, oranges, jicama, lemons, limes, cherry tomatoes, onions, garlic, green onions, chili peppers, iceberg lettuce, cucumbers, yams and sweet potatoes, snow peas, mushrooms, and zucchini. Snow peas are outstanding. On the sixth day of a backpacking trip they'll freshen up in cool water and be a crisp, green addition to pilaf, soup, or a grain salad.

If you start your trip with a small head of cabbage, a couple of avocados hard as baseballs, a fresh onion, and fresh jalapeño peppers, on the sixth day you can serve a big Mexican dinner: tostadas garnished with crisp cabbage and onions and luscious, ripe avocados complete with tortillas, refried beans, rice, and salsa. (See the recipe for *Mexican Chicken Tostadas* on page 185.)

Iceberg lettuce was developed by the agricultural industry to keep for a long time—from truck farm to supermarket. The way I package iceberg lettuce is an exception to the rule of never packaging veggies in plastic. Wrap a strip of several paper towels around the unwashed, uncut head of lettuce. Slightly dampen the paper towels with cold water, then put it all in a plastic bag and slip that into a ziploc freezer bag. The bag is then your salad bowl; a large ziploc works for up to four people, larger groups larger bags. We've eaten iceberg lettuce salads four days out that were wonderfully crisp and crunchy. Fresh cabbage and lettuce are admittedly heavy foods for backpacking, but a refreshing salad after a few days on the trail is such a special treat that I think the extra weight is worth it.

We can't carry a lot of fresh vegetables, because they weigh a lot, but it's amazing how satisfying even a small amount can be. Most of us crave crunchy vegetables after a few days in the backcountry, and a dinner with a small carrot-and-raisin salad becomes a special occasion. After days without fresh fruit, just the sight of bright green kiwi fruit slices is enough to lift our spirits, and a little bite is a wonderful treat.

A melon may sound ridiculously heavy for a backpacking trip, but a small cantaloupe is quite manageable if you eat it early in the trip. Chilled in the stream, sliced, and served wrapped in proscuitto—for breakfast or as a dinner hors d'oeuvre—it is food for the gods.

To avoid crushing weight, use fresh produce in small amounts. Combine it with dry staples and home-dried or freeze-dried food—and of course plan your menus according to how long your foods will keep.

Take advantage of natural refrigeration on the trail too. Early in the season you can often find a snowbank. A mountain stream is perfect for keeping food cold. A net bag like the kind oranges come in can be used to keep food in the stream. You can put things like cherry tomatoes, leftovers, and packages of cream cheese in large widemouth nalgene bottles, screw them tightly shut and put them in the net bag. Pesto in its nalgene bottle will last over a week if you can keep it in a cold stream part of the time. Wet vegetables will deteriorate, but you can protect veggies and other food from getting wet by double- or triple-bagging them in knotted plastic garbage bags (press out as much air as possible), putting the waterproof bag into the net bag, and lowering it into the icy water. Anchor the bag to a rock or a tree, or you'll lose it. If you're in bear country, don't forget to get your refrigerated food out of the stream and hang it with the rest of the food at night.

Finally, don't take chances with any food you suspect might be spoiled. Any cooked food than has been left sitting in the sun should be thrown away. If food has the least "off" odor, don't eat it. Even if it doesn't smell funny, put it in the garbage if you're in the least suspicious.

Step-By-Step Packaging Of a One-Day Menu

Now we'll go through the packing process for the following one-day menu step-by-step. This menu is for four people—two men and two women. It may guide you in figuring amounts too. I've included quantities and weights as well as packing information. The food for this day weighs about 10 pounds 6 ounces, or slightly over 2½ pounds per person.

Breakfast

Buttermilk Cornbread
Raspberry jam, butter
Sweet Potato Hash Browns, fresh onion
Coffee

Follow the "At home" recipe directions for *Buttermilk Cornbread* on page 132 and combine all dry ingredients and put in a plastic bag labeled "Sat. Brkfst. Cornbread. Add appx 1 cup H₂O & ⅓ cup oil, steam in buttered 3-qt pot for 30 min." Then double-bag it. The ⅓ cup oil has been figured into the main supply (when you looked over the menu and figured your amounts earlier as explained on page 30).

Put 6 ounces of home-dried sweet potatoes into a self-sealing bag with a small onion and label it "Sat Brk. Sweet Potato Hash Browns. Use ½ the onion for dinner tonite." (Another 2 TB oil for cooking the hash browns was figured into the total amount.) Both the cornbread mix and the sweet potato package are put into a ziploc with a "Sat. Brkfst" label.

Raspberry jam (6 oz) is put into a wide-mouth nalgene bottle and labelled "Raspberry Jam. Sat. Brkfst & Lunch." A half cube (2 oz) of butter is included with the main supply in a wide- mouth nalgene bottle. ¼ cup dry milk, 4 sugar cubes, and 1 cup coffee are added to the main supply. Breakfast weighs about 2 pounds 8 ounces.

Lunch

Leftover cornbread, raspberry jam
Cheese
Crackers
Carrots
Prunes and sunflower seeds

Everyone will be given their lunch at the beginning of the trip; lunch food is pretty obvious, and since everyone carries their own lunch I don't label it. Included in each person's lunches for this day are about 3 ounces cheese (bagged in a ziploc), 2 ounces crackers (ziploc), a medium carrot (brown paper bag), and ½ cup prunes and sunflower seeds (ziploc). After breakfast each person gets leftover cornbread spread with jam for their lunch, too. Lunches weigh about ¾ pound per person (not counting breakfast leftovers).

Dinner

Mexican Chicken Tostadas with:
    Fantastic Foods Refried Beans
    Avocado
    Cabbage
    Dry jack cheese
    Fresh onion
    Salsa
    Tabasco sauce
Minute Rice
Kiwi fruit slices
Mexican Chocolate

The Fantastic Foods Refried Beans are taken out of their box and bagged in a ziploc with the recipe cut from the box (with rounded corners—sharp corners puncture plastic bags). It's labeled "Sat. Din. Refried Beans."

Three cups of Minute Rice are measured into a self-sealing bag and a label affixed: "Sat Din. Minute Rice. Add to 3 cups boiling H2O. Stir, cover & remove from heat. Ready in about 5 min."

Dry jack cheese (6 oz) is put into a ziploc labeled "Sat Din. Cheese for tostadas." The 7-oz can of salsa is labeled "Sat Din." The beans, rice, cheese, and salsa are all put into a larger bag labeled "Sat. Nite Mexican Dinner."

The avocado, small cabbage, and 2 mild chilies are put into three brown paper bags and the bags are marked "Sat. Din. avocado," "Sat. Din. cabbage," and "Sat Din. chilies." The one-half fresh onion left over from breakfast will be used on the tostadas and in the *Mexican Chicken Tostada* sauce.

Eight tostada shells are bagged in a ziploc and carried in a cooking pot for protection. Include Tabasco sauce in the spice bag.

A Seal-A-Meal spice packet is made for *Mexican Chicken Tostadas*: 1 tsp cumin, ½ tsp oregano, 1 TB chili powder, 1 oz dried onions. The dehydrated tomato paste is put in another packet along with 2 cloves fresh garlic (unpeeled at this point). The can of chicken is labeled "Sat. Din." Two TB cooking oil were factored into the main supply. The spice packet, the can of chicken, and tomato sauce packet are all put in a larger ziploc bag labeled "Sat. Din. Chicken Tostadas. Sauté mild chilies & spices in 2 TB oil. Add garlic, minced. Then add tomato, chick. Then add 1-2 cups H2O gradually, cook about 10 min."

Four packages Swiss Miss Hot Chocolate mix are added to the main supply. Cinnamon for Mexican Chocolate is included in the spice bag. A fresh kiwi fruit is put in a brown paper bag to ripen, and carried in a cooking pot. This dinner weighs 4 pounds 12 ounces.

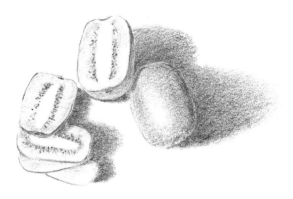

Equipment Checklist for the Backpacker's Kitchen

Stove
Fuel bottles
Pour spout/funnel
Stove repair kit
Pots and Pans:
Coffee pot (5- or 9-cup)
Aluminum or stainless steel pots with bail handles
and lids (3-, 4- and/or 10-quart size)
Nonstick aluminum frying pan (8- or 10-inch)
Miscellaneous Cooking Utensils:
Swiss Army knife (includes can opener, knife, cork-
screw)
Large kitchen spoon
Pancake turner
Wooden spoon
Whisk, grater, other extras
Heat diffuser
Pot gripper
Baking on the Trail:
Banks Frybake Pan or BakePacker or two nesting
pots (such as a 3-quart nesting in a 9-quart)
Personal Eating Utensils:
Cup
Plate/bowl
Soup spoon, fork
Miscellaneous Supplies:
Nylon screen/orange net bag
Cord for clothesline, rope for bearbagging
**Kitchen Bag—A ziploc bag containing all or some of
the following:**
Small pot scrubber
Biodegradable soap
Wooden matches or lighter
Heavy-duty aluminum foil (a few folded squares)
Paper towels (a few folded squares)
Hot pad or mitt
Bandana and/or dishtowel
Clothespins
Large heavy-duty garbage bags
Water Filter
Water Containers:
Water bottle
Collapsible bucket/Watersack/Reliance collapsible
containers
13-gallon white plastic garbage bags
Headlamp

6

Kitchen Equipment and Supplies

Novices sometimes buy the cutest and most useless items the store has to offer. Among the gadgets and doodads you don't need to spend money on are mess kits, facile-but-fragile stoves, fire starter kits, inflatable sinks, pocket saws, 4-ounce foil packets of "Purified, Sterilized, Emergency Drinking Water," elaborate first aid kits, and emergency survival kits containing C-rations and smoke bombs that will, as the directions tell us, "produce an immense volume of orange smoke visible for many miles."

When buying your kitchen equipment start with simple equipment and think multiple use. One 3-quart pot, for example, is far more practical than a one of those little mess kits with doll-size pots and pans. You'll be able to use the larger pot for fetching water, bathing, washing dishes, and carrying crushable food in your pack, and it does all kinds of cooking jobs for up to six people. For your first trip you might want buy one 3-quart pot and use equipment you already have in your kitchen at home, or possibly see what you can find in a thrift store. Then after you've been on a trip or two you'll have a more realistic idea of what you need and you can really get into the fun of outfitting yourself with quality equipment.

The kitchen equipment checklist at the beginning of the chapter is meant to be used as a guide, and this chapter tells you about the equipment and supplies listed.

The kitchen equipment you bring on your trip depends on the size of your party, your menu, and your itinerary (although the number of stoves, pots and pans you need remains about the same whether you go out for a weekend or ten days).

A party of four peakbaggers eating simply and striving for super-light packs might bring only one stove, fuel, a stove repair kit, and one 4-quart pot, and each person would have a Swiss Army knife, a cup, and a spoon. The list for a couple planning to bake on the trail might be: one stove, fuel and repair kit, one 5-cup coffee pot, one 3-quart pot and nesting 1-quart pot, one 8-inch non-stick aluminum frying pan, one kitchen spoon, one pancake turner, Swiss Army knife, miscellaneous items, and personal eating utensils: spoon, cup, plate or bowl.

A group of 12 to 15 planning to make a base camp and cook more elaborate meals might bring: three or four stoves with fuel and repair kit, two large coffee pots, three 3-quart pots, one 10-quart pot, two frying pans, and all the miscellaneous items on the list. It's usually a good idea to bring a second stove when there are more than four people in the wilderness party.

Stoves

Today there are simply too many of us using the wilderness to use precious firewood for cooking, and it is accepted by every thinking person who goes into the backcountry that cooking will be done on a stove—not a campfire. A stove has become as essential to the backpacker as a warm sleeping bag.

Although most of us use stoves in the interests of low-impact camping, it's in fact easier to cook on a stove than on a campfire. With a stove you have an adjustable flame, you can cook in any weather conditions, you don't have to gather wood, you never have to fuss with lighting wet wood—and when it's time to wash dishes you don't have to reckon with sooty, blackened pots.

Every recipe in this book is designed to be cooked on a little one-burner backpacking stove—and with the right pan you can even bake breads.

Selecting a Stove

What kind of stove is right for you? This is the first and most important question to be settled regarding your kitchen equipment.

There are two types of backpacking stoves: pressurized gas-burning and liquid-fuel-burning. In North America that means either a butane (pressurized gas) or a white gas (liquid-fuel) stove. In other parts of the world white gas is not available, so some stove manufacturers make multifuel models. These stoves can burn both white gas and kerosene, and some models are capable of burning everything from automobile gas to cleaning fluid!

If you're a summer backpacker using your stove for only a few hours each season, a simple butane stove may be the answer. If you'll use your stove for snow camping, at high altitudes, or for international travel, or if you just want a high-performance stove, your choice should be one of the liquid-fuel-burning stoves.

Other points to consider when buying a stove are fuel efficiency, flame adjustability, stability of both stove and pots, and ease of repair in the field. For information on stove safety and maintenance, techniques for conserving fuel, and cooking methods on a backpacking stove see the next chapter.

There are several excellent stoves on the market ranging in cost from about $25 to almost $100. A few of the more popular models are reviewed here. Weights and boiling times were provided by the stove repairmen at the Berkeley REI store. Stove weights are without fuel, and boiling times start with one quart of 70-degree water at sea level in still air.

Butane Stoves

Stoves fueled by butane are easy to use. You light them by simply turning a knob and holding a match to the burner. Fuel comes in disposable cartridges, so you don't have to go to the trouble of filling a fuel tank. Unfortunately, butane gas doesn't burn very hot. There's an obvious difference in the heat output of white gas and butane stoves, and at high elevations butane sputters and stalls. In cold weather (temperatures under 30 degrees) the pressurized gas turns to liquid and you must devise a way to keep cartridges warm, as with your body heat.

Empty fuel cartridges must, of course, be packed out of the backcountry. Two other disadvantages of the butane stoves are that usually the fuel cartridge can't be changed until all the fuel is used up, and that when fuel runs low the resulting low pressure inside the cartridge means decreased heat output.

Nevertheless, many people prefer the easy-to-use butane stove. If you decide to buy one, be certain that fuel cartridges to fit it are widely available.

Gaz C-206 Bleuet

This reliable stove has been on the market for many years, and fuel cartridges are available throughout the United States, Canada, Africa, and Europe. However, the Bleuet takes a long 8½ minutes to bring a quart of water to a boil. At 11.6 ounces it's lightweight, but since it's not terribly fuel-efficient you have to carry a bit more weight in cartridges. The Bleuet has a low price tag and is an excellent value at about $25.

MSR Rapidfire

Mountain Safety Research now makes a butane stove, as well as their white gas and multifuel models. The Rapidfire burns cartridges of isobutane, which burns hotter than butane because the can is under higher pressure—it takes only 4½ minutes to bring a quart of water to a boil. Another attribute of the Rapidfire is the self-sealing fuel canister. Unlike most pressurized-gas stoves, you can disconnect the Rapidfire from its canister each time after you use it. The Rapidfire has the same design and excellent stability of the MSR Whisperlite; both cartridges and stove cost considerably more than the Bleuet.

White Gas And Multifuel Stoves

White gas stoves are the choice of most experienced backcountry travelers. White gas is highly flammable and burns hot—a white gas stove can bring a quart of water to a boil in three to four minutes.

Liquid fuel stoves are definitely more difficult to light—they must be primed or pumped—but all things considered the butane stove seems almost like a toy when compared to the high performance liquid-fuel stove. And once you get to know your stove, lighting it is no problem at all. In fact, we hard-core backpackers get attached to our little one-burner stoves and lighting them becomes second nature to us. We take comfort in the sound one makes when running well and we know instinctively when it needs refueling.

It seems that everyone has a favorite stove and no other kind will do. One stove may be very lightweight, another a bit heavier but with other features to recommend it.

Coleman Feather 400

This stove was introduced in 1990. It's basically Coleman's old-reliable Peak 1 with a new name and some improvements. The new stove is 6 ounces lighter and has a single-lever control, and the generator has been upgraded. I've used the Peak 1 for many years, and it's a sturdy, stable, reliable little workhorse with a high heat output. My stove is in use on trips all summer—often at altitudes of 12,000 feet—and for some snow camping trips in the winter, and it stands up well to heavy use. It's a self-cleaning stove so there's no complicated cleaning procedure. Another great feature is its flame adjustability; you can turn the flame down to a barely visible simmer and it won't go out. This stove is fuel-efficient anyway, but I think the simmer capability results in saving a considerable amount of fuel. The Feather 400 has the lowest price tag of the liquid-fuel stoves reviewed here; priced at around $40, it's one of the best values in camping equipment today. It takes 3.4 minutes to bring a quart of water to a boil, and weighs 26 ounces.

**Peak 1
Multifuel**

This is a smaller and lighter-weight stove than the Coleman Feather 400. It burns white gas or kerosene and is more expensive than the Feather 400, about $60. White gas brings a quart of water to a boil in 3.9 minutes, kerosene in 4.1 minutes. Weight 18 oz.

**MSR
Whisperlite**

I have owned two Whisperlites. They're lightweight and stable, and have good heat output. They're good when it's cold, too. One morning I brushed several inches of snow off my Whisperlite, and it started with the first match. However, I'm sorry to say that my Whisperlites haven't been consistently reliable. Also, after each use the Whisperlite should be cleaned with a tiny needle-like tool, and I find this a tedious operation. The Whisperlite runs well on high and medium, but tends to go out if turned down very low. Whisperlites are designed to fold up to be stowed in a small space, and the fuel bottle attaches to the stove to become the fuel tank. This design makes for compactness and light weight, but I don't like the bother of putting together and dismantling my stove at each new camp. Nevertheless, many people swear by this stove. It boils a quart of water in 3.8 minutes, and is the lightest of the liquid-fuel stoves, 12.7 oz.

**MSR
Whisperlite
Internationale**

This is like the Whisperlite, but burns white gas and kerosene. Both kerosene and white gas bring a quart of water to boil in about 4 minutes. Weight 12 oz.

MSR XGK This is the stove that burns just about everything but water: white gas, kerosene, leaded and unleaded automobile fuel, aviation fuel, #1 stove oil, diesel, and Stoddard cleaning solvent! This excellent, high-powered stove is designed for international expeditions where it's necessary to melt snow at elevations of 15,000 feet plus. It's the most expensive of the stoves reviewed here. People who do a lot of snow camping make good use of the XGK, too. The XGK has just two speeds: high and off. White gas brings a quart of water to a boil in 3.4 minutes, kerosene in 3 minutes. Weight: 18.4 oz.

SVEA 123/ Optimus 8R These two stoves look different, but they're the same stove in different formats and are made by the same company. Both have been favorites of backpackers for many years and each has a reputation for being completely reliable. Long-time users describe these stoves as "bomb-proof," and report they hold a simmer with no problem. The SVEA 123 is made of brass and comes with a windscreen and a small cooking pot. Weight: 18 oz. The Optimus 8R comes in a blue metal box and the lid serves as a wind screen. Weight: 25 oz. Both stoves bring a quart of water to a boil in 4.1 minutes.

Fuel Bottles White gas must be carried in a strong, leakproof container. Both Sigg and MSR make quality lightweight aluminum fuel bottles. (Since the fuel bottle is also the fuel tank with MSR stoves, the company warns their stove users to use the MSR fuel bottle exclusively.)

Pour Spouts A pour spout or a funnel for filling stove tanks should be carried as well. REI makes an ingenious cap that fits on Sigg and MSR bottles and can be turned to pour or closed.

Stove Repair Kits Most stove manufacturers sell their own stove repair kits, and it's smart to carry one. I carry a minature wrench made especially for the Peak 1, a pair of small snub-nose pliers, and a few spare parts.

Pots and Pans

A good starter set for your pots and pans would be one 3-quart pot (or two nesting pots, 2-quart and 4-quart), a coffee pot (if brewing coffee), and a nonstick aluminum frying pan. Avoid cook kits with frying pans that lack a nonstick coating, thimble-sized coffee cups, bowls in a variety of sizes, and other items you don't want or need. It's usually better to buy equipment separately rather than in sets—that way you'll get exactly what you want.

Make sure your pots have snug lids. A covered pot cooks food faster and conserves fuel. I favor pots with bail handles, the kind that can be made to stand straight up over the pot. This feature helps you avoid burned fingers, and with the bail up, you can quickly lift a pot off the fire if it starts to boil over.

If you get your pots from a thrift store, a discount store, or someplace other than a camping store, make sure you can live with the handles. Pots with big intrusive handles aren't practical for camp cooking and take up precious room in your pack. Some camping pots are designed without handles and are to be used with pot grabbers. You may want to cut the handles off thrift store pots and use with a pot grabber. The pot grabber system works fine and probably saves a bit in weight, but it is more trouble than pots with bail handles.

Aluminum or Stainless Steel?

What material should your camp cookware be made of? Pots and pans suitable for backpacking and cooking on the trail are usually made of aluminum or stainless steel.

I think aluminum pots work best. Aluminum is extremely light-weight, has good heat conductivity, and food doesn't stick or burn easily.

However, we are seeing more and more stainless steel being used these days for camping utensils. Stainless steel is beautiful and shiny, and cleans easily—but I don't think that it's the best material for backpacking cookpots. Stainless steel is heavy, and it has poor heat conductivity. The good stainless steel pots and pans found in home kitchens are heavy gauge and have an inner core of aluminum or heavy-gauge copper to increase heat conduction. Such pots are too heavy to be practical for backpacking, so stainless steel pots for camping are made of a thinner gauge, which leads to hot spots and burned food.

Sticking and burning has been my experience with stainless steel camp cookware, but many people who are buying the new pots report that they like cooking in their stainless steel, even though it weighs more. And they especially like the easy cleaning. In addition, many people feel that eating food cooked in aluminum pots isn't healthful—there is a widely held belief that eating food cooked in aluminum can cause Alzheimer's disease. Most campers that I talked to say they now use stainless steel because they feel it's unhealthy to eat food cooked in aluminum. One woman's response was typical: "I trashed my aluminum pots because I heard it causes Alzheimer's."

Actually, this is a matter of some debate. Most studies show there is no scientific evidence to support this theory, but other studies imply there may be a connection between Alzheimer's and aluminum pots. Given that most people use their camp cook pots for only a few hours each year, I'm not convinced that this should be a big issue—but as long as the question remains, it appears that people will continue to abandon aluminum and go for the heavier, more expensive stainless-steel cooking pots.

I do have an expensive three-piece camp cookware set of stainless steel. These pots are fine for boiling water, making pasta and heating thin soups, but foods of thicker texture like beans, spaghetti sauce, and rice tend to stick and burn unless carefully watched.

I'm waiting for a manufacturer to come out with backpacking pots and pans made of lightweight aluminum with a tough, anodized nonstick coating so that food doesn't come in direct contact with the metal. In the meantime, if you object to eating food cooked in aluminum, your best choice is probably stainless steel. Get the kind with copper-clad bottoms because copper aids heat conduction. If your stainless steel sticks and burns, try using an aluminum heat diffuser from a hardware store.

Coffee Pots   Most camp coffee pots are made of aluminum. The best kind have a double metal wire handle on the side and a bail handle that can stand straight up over the pot.

Frying Pans   Get an 8- or 10-inch nonstick aluminum frying pan with a handle that folds into the pan and takes up minimum pack space. Another alternative is the non-stick heavier gauge aluminum Banks Frybake Pan which doubles as a frying pan and a mini-oven and comes with a pot grabber and a lid. See *Baking on the Trail* below for more details on the Frybake Pan.

Miscella-neous Cooking Utensils   You probably don't need all the items listed below. Eliminate what you can considering your menu. Weight is always a concern, but it's also good not to have too many *things* in your pack. Several of these cooking tools can be bought at hardware stores.

Pocket Knife   I don't go into the backcountry without my trusty Swiss Army knife. It provides a can opener, a screwdriver, scissors, even tweezers and a toothpick, and does all kinds of kitchen jobs. The Victorinox brand is the best. Because I do a lot of cooking on my trips, I also bring along a good paring knife. It's made by Opinel and comes in several sizes; the one I use has a 3½-inch blade, weighs only 1½ ounces, and is reasonably priced.

Spoon, Pancake Turner

Spoons and pancake turners made of lightweight nylon are good choices for your backcountry kitchen, and you'll want to use plastic utensils on some nonstick pans anyway. A wooden spoon is a light yet strong cooking tool. If you're cooking for a group you may want more sturdy utensils. A large metal spoon with a long handle is fine for big groups. If you're striving for light weight, just bring a pancake turner; it does most cooking jobs, your cup makes a good soup ladle, and you can use your soup spoon for everything else.

Whisk, Grater

You can find tiny metal whisks in outdoor and hardware stores, but a larger white plastic whisk found in kitchen specialty shops is more effective and much lighter. Some cooks bring tiny graters for carrots, cheese, and potatoes.

Potgrabber

A small aluminum potgrabber weighs only one ounce. A longer, more deluxe model made by Scott Manufacturing Company can be purchased with the Banks Frybake Pan and weighs 4 ounces. Tip: if you continually misplace your camouflage-gray pot grabber while cooking, wrap one handle with red cord to make it easier to spot.

Heat Diffuser

A heat diffuser is made of aluminum, weighs 6½ ounces, and costs about $2 at hardware stores. If your stainless steel pots tend to stick, you may find it useful. A heat diffuser can help you turn out a better baked product with the mini-oven method if you don't have a stove with simmer capability.

Baking On the Trail

If you want to make baked goods on the trail, there are two baking methods, requiring different pot systems. For more details on baking see *Baking on a Backpacking Stove* in the next chapter.

Steaming

The BakePacker is a 9-ounce aluminum ring 2-inches high and 7⅜ inches in diameter with a steaming rack inside. It fits inside a 3-quart pot and you bake in a food-safe plastic bag or roasting bag at boiling water temperatures. This nifty little system works well for quick breads, cakes, and muffins, and you don't have to scrub out the pot because both mixing and baking are done in the bag. However, because you can never get a higher temperature than the boiling point of water, you can't bake things like brownies and dense breads; also note that some of the pre-packaged commercial mixes which are recommended in the cookbook pamphlet that comes with it taste awfully empty. The BakePacker is available through REI and Campmor; see *Mail-Order Sources* in the appendix.

You can also use the two-pot system for baking with the steaming method. You need two pots of different sizes with tightly fitting lids. One pot nests inside the other with at least a half inch to spare around the sides. For four servings, you'll need a 1- to 1½-quart pot nesting in a 3-quart pot; for larger groups, a 10-quart pot with a nesting 3-quart pot is best.

Mini-Ovens

For baking with the mini-oven method, it's important to have a stove you can turn down to simmer. If your stove is capable of running with a low flame you may be able to bake with this method using a heat diffuser, but if your stove runs only at medium or high heat, you will burn anything you attempt to bake.

To put together your own mini-oven you'll need a frying pan at least two inches deep with a snug-fitting, flat lid on which you can build a small twig fire.

I use the Banks Frybake Pan. It's designed for the mini-oven method of baking and is a quality piece of equipment. It can give baking results like a real oven, and it doubles as a frying pan. It's a heavier-gauge aluminum pan with a tough, stick-resistant anodized coating that you can use with metal utensils. It comes with a ridged, domed lid. You build a twig fire on the lid and turn your stove down to simmer to create a mini-oven. Once you get the hang of it, it bakes delicious biscuits, brownies, yeast breads, pizza, quick breads, and casseroles. This baking system is faster and uses far less fuel than the water-temperature baking method. There are two models: The Alpine is 8" x 2" high and weighs 13 oz. The Expedition is 10½" x 2" and weighs 29.4 oz. See *Mail-Order Sources* in the appendix for ordering details.

Personal Eating Utensils

Some people like simple chopsticks and a bowl; others want a big plate and stainless steel silverware. You need a cup for soup and hot beverages, and some people even eat their meals from a cup. Metal Sierra cups are popular, but metal cups inevitably cause burned lips, and hot drinks cool rapidly in metal cups. The sloping sides of the Sierra cup are good if you want your cup to double as a bowl/plate, but they make it easy to spill liquids. Your cup should also double as a measuring cup; a 16 ounce plastic measuring cup with a handle is a good mug; it won't burn your lips and it will keep your drinks warm. Plastic thermos cups and insulated cups with measuring cup marks are good choices, too. Whatever your choice, you'll be glad if you have a *big* cup.

It makes sense to bring a plastic bowl or a plastic plate, but you don't need both. A flat plate—rather than the compartmentalized-type reminiscent of airline meals—is versatile. You can roll out biscuits or pizza dough on it, protected by a paper towel it works as a cutting board, and it slides easily into the map pocket of your pack.

For eating utensils, a soup spoon and a fork will do, and some people bring only a soup spoon. Stainless steel and sturdy, lightweight Lexan are good choices, but a 4-piece service isn't necessary; you can leave the knife (you have your pocket knife) and small teaspoon at home.

If you're backpacking with a group it's a good idea to mark your plate, cup and cutlery so they don't get mixed up with others. I use fingernail polish.

Water Filters

Filters are one method of purifying water, and they have the advantage of leaving water tasting pure and sweet. I have used three of the filters on the market. The Swiss-made Katadyn filter is a beautifully made, efficient piece of equipment that will last a lifetime. It's made for international travel and its 0.2 micron ceramic filter screens out giardia and just about any bacteria, fungi or protozoa that exists. The filter can be cleaned several hundred times; a replacement filter costs $90, and the Katadyn itself costs a steep $200—but before you decide to run out and stock up on iodine, take a look at two lower-priced filter pumps.

The First Need costs about $40 and pumps approximately 50 to 100 quarts of water before you need to replace the $24 filter. It has a 0.4 micron charcoal-based filter which strains out not only giardia and other "bugs" but pesticides and many other chemicals as well.

The Timberline costs about $25 and pumps up to 400 quarts of water before needing a new $12 filter. The Timberline has only a 2 micron filter. It's an adequate, low cost pump for mountain backpacking in the United States, but would not protect you against many organisms found in the tropics and other parts of the world. I own and use both the First Need and Timberline pumps and like them both. In 12 years of leading wilderness trips, not one person on my trips has ever gotten giardia. When using any filter pump, its best to pump water from settled water in a pot or bucket in order to avoid clogging the filter with algae or sand. Also, it pays to buy the pre-filter that fits your water filter; it strains out coarse debris and will greatly extend the life of your filter.

Water Bottles

Few things are more irritating than a leaky water bottle, so buy a good one. Nalgene wide-mouth 1-liter bottles with attached lids are excellent. My preference is a biker's water bottle. Designed to be used while pedaling down the highway, it's a "one-handed" water bottle with a nipple top that can be opened and closed with your teeth, and on hot days you can cool yourself off with a squirt of water.

Water Containers

A handy yellow plastic collapsible bucket goes with me on every trip. It weighs 9½ ounces, holds 2½ gallons of water, and costs little.

The 4-ounce, compact Watersack holds 3 gallons of water and you can buy a showerhead attachment for it, too.

The Reliance collapsible water containers are serviceable, but I don't advise getting the large 5-gallon size because the large size springs leaks easily—the weight of the full 5 gallons of water, 40 pounds, makes it more susceptible to punctures. The smaller sizes make it easier to carry water from stream to camp, too.

Miscellaneous Supplies

One of the handiest kitchen items in my pack is a simple piece of nylon screen from the hardware store. I usually take two pieces of different sizes; together they weigh only 12 ounces (and you'll probably want smaller pieces than I need for my trips). The smaller piece is a 3' x 3' square. It performs many jobs including draining pasta and protecting prepared food from insects, and a corner of it makes a good pot scrubber.

From the larger piece I make a camp cupboard perfect for storing dishes for a large group on base camp trips or for car camping. For groups I use a 3' x 6' piece, but you can cut yours to any size. Fold the screen in half lengthwise, and with the fold down fasten the raw edges together onto a clothesline with clothespins. This makes a long, open tube. Put dishes in either end; it holds dishes, cups, silverware, even pots and pans. They dry quickly in their open-air cupboard, they're protected from dirt and insects, and you can tell at a glance where your dish is. Sometimes I feel like the Heloise of the wilderness.

A net orange bag does pretty much the same job as nylon screen. You can use it for keeping food cold in the creek, storing dishes, and hanging food. On our yearly 10-day trip to Kauai, orange bags and nylon screen are indispensible for hanging ripening fruit and vegetables and storing other food.

The contents of your kitchen bag—pot scrubber, soap, matches, and so on will shrink or expand according to the size of your group and your cooking needs. A bandana has many uses: a hot pad, a napkin, a dish towel, and more. I carry at least two bandanas on every trip. A lighter—or wooden matches stowed in a waterproof miniature nalgene bottle—is a necessity. You don't need paper towels, but a just a few are handy. Heavy-duty aluminum foil has many uses. Take two or three folded squares and re-use it throughout the trip. You can use it for heating breads, keeping food warm, and wrapping leftover food; it makes a makeshift serving dish and a good windscreen for your stove.

The 13-gallon white garbage bags, or even large ziplocs, are handy for carrying garbage. I bring large, heavy-duty garbage bags for covering my pack and protecting other gear if it rains. And a big garbage bag makes a wonderful solar-heated bathtub after a few dirty days on the trail: Put about 6-8 gallons of water in a big black garbage bag and let it sit in full sun for 3 or 4 hours. When the water's hot, crawl in and enjoy a warm bath!

Finally, although it's not really a kitchen item, a headlamp instead of a hand-held flashlight will leave both hands free for cooking after dark. However you try to avoid it, you will at some time in your backpacking career end up cooking in the dark. My favorite type of headlamp has batteries in front instead of in back; that way you can read in your sleeping bag without having to rest your head on a hard battery case.

7

Cooking In the Wilderness

The Low-Impact Campsite

Wilderness living requires a different way of thinking from our everyday lives in the city, and minimizing our impact on the wilderness is a primary consideration. If we think of ourselves as guests in the wilderness, I think that many of the do's and don'ts of wilderness living become more clear to us.

Setting Up Camp

It should be your aim to camp and leave no trace that you have been there. You should, however, make your camp in an already-established site unless the site is overused.

When setting up the backcountry kitchen, be certain to camp at least 200' from water sources and try to take a different route each time you fetch water in order to avoid making a trail to the water.

Avoid camping on grassy areas. When setting up camp, I often see people in a frenzy of "housecleaning" activity clearing an area by scraping away pine needles and leaves with their feet. This is not acceptable; leave ground cover as it is—scraping an area down to the soil makes a dirty and over-used campsite.

Washing Up   Wash dishes in hot water in a cooking pot with
biodegradable soap and rinse well; cold water is
fine for rinsing. Wash dishes and rinse dishes 200'
back from lakes and streams, and don't ever put
soap (even biodegradable soap) in streams or lakes.
Dispose of cooking and dishwater well away from
camp and water sources. Disperse water widely
and in a different place each time. Food scraps from
dishwater and cooking should be packed out.

If you want to bathe or shampoo, lather and rinse
at least 200' from lakes and streams. Keeping your
hands clean if you're handling food becomes even
more important in the wilderness. With groups, it's
a good idea to keep soap, a fingernail brush, and a
small metal bowl near the kitchen, and anyone
handling food—especially if returning from a trip
to the woods—washes her hands or the entire wilderness party runs the risk of getting sick with
Backpacker's Revenge. Wash your hands with soap
and warm water, and don't simply rinse hands off
in the stream (and possibly contaminate the stream
as well).

Campfires   Campfires are discouraged but if you do have a
campfire, you can burn paper and some other garbage. Be aware that foil does not burn and is in hot
chocolate wrappers, instant soups, and other food
wrappers that look like only paper on the outside.
If these things do get thrown into the campfire
you'll have to fish them out, a tedious and dirty job.
Be judicious with the burning of non-paper trash;
complete cremation is difficult with things like
large plastic bags and citrus peels. Before leaving
camp put out campfire thoroughly and make sure
all garbage is thoroughly burned.

Just before leaving, walk around camp with a plastic bag in hand and pick up even the tiniest scraps:
pieces of foil, burned matches, little paper-covered
wires used to close plastic bags. Leave your camp
cleaner than you found it.

Keeping Food Safe from Animal Bandits

If you have food left over, don't bury it or leave it for animals to eat—pack it out. Human food is not good for wild animals' digestive systems. Moreover, once backpackers' food becomes a part of their menu wild animals become marauding pests. I've noticed that many of the marmots on the east side of Mt. Whitney have scruffy tails and unhealthy-looking coats. These marmots are professional bandits, and I wonder if their diet of trail mix and freeze-dried food is the cause.

Given the slightest opportunity, bears and raccoons and other varmints will raid your food supply. Just because you don't see any animals don't assume that they're not around. Most of these raiders are nocturnal, and they are unbelievably clever—especially bears. Bears can recognize a camp cooler or a backpack through a car window, and stories from Yellowstone National Park tell of bears that have learned to pop open the doors of the airtight Volkswagen by bouncing on the roof. Never underestimate the cleverness of a bear.

You can be relatively casual if you're hanging your food to protect it from varmints. Toss a rope over a tree branch, haul your food bag up, tie up the other end and get a good night's sleep. But if you're in bear country, food must be hung by the counterbalance method from steel cables (provided in some wilderness areas) or from a tree branch. (See the counterbalance method illustration on the next page.) If you're hanging your food from a tree, the branch must be 4 to 5 inches in diameter, extend 10 feet out from the tree, and be about 20 feet up from the ground, and the branches around it should be very thin or very far away from your hanging branch. This is because Mama Bear will send Baby Bear up the tree and out onto branches that won't support her weight. I've heard stories of a bear taking a flying leap and slicing the bear bag open with his claws, and of one mama bear who climbed the tree and actually tossed her cub out at the bear bag! They got the food.

Black bears aren't after you—they just want your food—and you have to go to extraordinary lengths to protect it. If you're in an area where bears are a real problem, also put away with your food fragrant cosmetics, toothpaste and the clothes you've cooked in or other clothes that may smell of food. And whatever you do, don't take food to bed with you or keep food in your tent.

Some bears are so persistent and clever that I think an all-night "bear watch," is sometimes necessary along with the bearbagging. When the bear comes, flash lights, bang rocks on metal pots, and whoop like an Indian. The noise and light seem to weaken their resolve and they usually leave. We have done bear watches on my trips, taking turns in two or three hour shifts. So far I haven't lost any food to bears—but frankly, I don't sleep well in bear country.

Recently, the Forest Service and other government agencies that manage wilderness areas have started to place "bear boxes" in car campgrounds

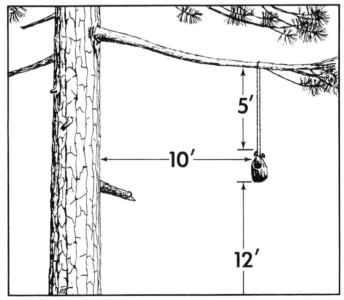

Recommended minimum distances for bearbagging on a tree branch

and also in some wilderness areas. The kind I've used is simply a large, heavy-duty metal footlocker with a latch that—so far—no bear has been able to figure out. This is good for humans because we don't lose our food and we get more sleep. It's especially good for bears because they'll go back to foraging for roots, berries, and other natural foods which promote a more healthful and peaceful bear lifestyle.

Giardia

Giardia lamblia, a parasite that can be present in the coldest, purest-looking rushing stream, has become more prevalent in our wilderness areas in the last ten years or so. Symptoms of an attack, which include flatulence, diarrhea, and vomiting, can take from three days to as long as a month to develop. We therefore must purify our water.

How to Purify Water

Boiling water for 5 minutes is the most effective way to purify water, but fuel is heavy, and obviously it isn't always practical to boil water, so we filter our drinking water or treat it with iodides.

Water Filters

Filter pumps are available from backpacking stores. A 0.4 micron filter keeps giardia cysts from passing through. Filter pumps weigh about 12 ounces, but there's the great advantage of having your drinking water taste sweet and pure. However, filter pumps can get clogged or break so I think it's a good idea always to bring a little iodine with you. For more information on filter pumps see *Chapter 6, **Kitchen Equipment and Supplies.***

Iodine

Iodides for purifying water are available in pills (one popular brand is Potable Aqua), iodine crystals (you buy the crystals in a brown glass bottle and mix up a concentrate which you add to your water), and ordinary 2% tincture of iodine (a liquid) which can be found in most drug stores. (Please note that halazone, bleach, and other so-called "water purifiers" that do not contain iodides are not effective against giardia.) Iodides are effective against giardia whether in pills, tincture, or crystal form—but ordinary 2% tincture of iodine is by far the least expensive.

Put ten drops (no more) of 2% tincture of iodine in a liter of water, wait for about 20 minutes, and the water is safe to drink. Make sure that you pour some treated water on the lid and mouth of your water bottle, too. A small amount of ascorbic acid (powdered vitamin C) added to iodized water— perhaps a teaspoon per liter—does a pretty fair job of masking the taste of the iodine; some people add lemonade mixes, too. If you do add something to your water, be certain that you add it *after* the 20 minutes have elapsed, because the vitamin C can counteract the effect of the iodides.

Most people report that iodine pills taste better than the 2% tincture. However, be aware that the pills start to oxidize when the bottle is opened, so pills from an old bottle that you have carried around from season to season are probably no longer effective. Also, be certain that the pills completely dissolve and that you mix the iodine into the solution instead of letting it sit in a yellow-brown cloud in the bottom of the bottle.

Since giardia can't live in air, it's not necessary to purify dishwater, just make sure dishes are dry before you use them. And of course pasta water, coffee and tea water, and any other water that you boil anyway doesn't need to be pumped or iodized, just boiled for 5 minutes.

Cooking On a Backpacking Stove

Whether you're at a party or out camping everybody likes to hang out in the kitchen. Set your stove up so that you can be social, but for safety keep it well away from traffic. The small one-burner backpacking stove is not a very stable base for cooking pots and they can tip off the stove with the slightest bump. Make sure your stove is solid and level. Cooking on a camp stove is a busy job, and the cook doesn't need the distraction of balancing pots of hot food on a rickety stove.

Usually I set my stove on the flat ground rather than perched on a waist-high rock where a pot might topple over and spill boiling water on someone. A stove set on the ground with a small, low wall of flat rocks around three sides will heat things faster and burn far less fuel than a more exposed stove. To conserve fuel, always put your stove in a place where it's protected from wind and where a bit of heat will be reflected back—but do take caution with wind screens. Unless you're using one designed specifically for your stove it's possible to have too much heat reflecting back on your stove and it can overheat—or even explode.

Avoid cooking in a tent if at all possible. It's messy, and it's quite probable that your stove could flare up and damage the tent. Moreover, running a stove in a closed tent can cause death by carbon-monoxide poisoning. If you're inside because of bad weather, try to wait for a break in the storm and cook outside. If the weather is really bad, the best solution is to set the stove up in the vestibule or just outside the door while you sit inside.

Fuel and Figuring Amounts

A Sigg aluminum liter bottle full of white gas weighs exactly two pounds. Fuel is heavy, so you must figure amounts needed as accurately as possible and do whatever you can to conserve fuel. You should know how long it takes your particular stove to boil a quart of water, the fuel tank capacity of your stove and how long a full tank of gas will burn at high heat. Stove notes that I keep for my stoves show that my Peak 1's fuel tank capacity is 1½ cups and a tank burns for about 1 hour and 20 minutes at high heat. Therefore, 1 liter burns for approximately 4 hours at high heat. When I'm figuring amounts, I look at my menu, estimate stove-running times for each meal and go from there. This is approximate at best, but it's a good place to start. (The very best measure I have for figuring fuel amounts is keeping notes on fuel use for each trip; I note how many people were on the trip and save the trip menus as well.)

Air temperature and altitude must be considered, too. At elevations above 9000' or 10,000' it takes longer to cook foods, so you must bring more fuel. For a three-day trip with 6 people I'd probably bring at least 2 additional cups of white gas, just to make sure. Stoves don't operate as efficiently as at sea level, either. Cold weather can mean finicky, fuel-gobbling stoves, and food will take longer to heat when the food and the air are cold.

For an easier, fuel-saving start in the morning in cold weather or at high altitude, take your stove to bed with you to keep it warm. Wrap it in a jacket or a towel and keep it warm in the bottom of your sleeping bag. Cold fuel doesn't start easily, so the stove should be filled with enough fuel to get you through breakfast; if you're using butane, keep the cartridge warm in your sleeping bag, too.

When filling liquid-fuel stoves, never top off your fuel tank. Most stoves don't run efficiently with too-full tanks, and they will often leak precious gas as well. Underfilling is best. Always use a funnel to fill liquid-fuel stoves to avoid spillage, and *always* replace the bottle lid just as soon as you've filled the stove. Do this not simply because white gas evaporates quickly, but also because Murphy's law applies here: If you forget to replace the lid, you'll knock over the fuel bottle.

If you're hiking from a lower to a higher altitude the pressure change can force fuel out of your stove. This happened to me on one trip when we were running low on fuel. The stove had been used for a short time at breakfast, so the tank had been pumped up. That day we hiked from 9500' to 12,000'; I smelled white gas while hiking, and discovered that we'd lost quite a bit of fuel. Now when going higher I remember to unscrew the fuel-tank cap and release the pressure (you'll hear a hissing sound as the air escapes), and also to keep under a half tank of fuel in my stoves.

Cooking
Techniques

Conserving heat conserves fuel. Always cook with lids on pots. This makes a dramatic difference in how long it takes foods to heat and liquids to boil, and in resulting fuel consumption.

You can heat bread by wrapping it in foil and placing it on the lid of a pot of hot food. If you're having a couple of courses and have to take one pot off the heat while you're cooking the other dish, you can keep food warm by wrapping it in a jacket or a towel. Keep pots of hot food close together, and stack cooking pots if it's not too precarious. If we're having more than one course, I usually have flat rocks arranged so that I can put warm food in covered cubbyholes to help keep it warm.

For shorter cooking time, rehydrate dried foods longer. Start rehydrating in the afternoon if possible—dried foods will take far less time to cook. Pasta must be cooked quickly in furiously boiling water, but some foods, like small orange lentils, can be cooked for about 15 minutes and then left in a warm place for a while to finish cooking. Instead of cooking on the stove for 15 or 20 minutes, bulgur can be covered with boiling water and allowed to sit for an hour—it will cook completely.

A white-gas stove with the ability to simmer is a big fuel-saver and will help you avoid cooking disasters like burned food and lumpy sauces. In stove-comparison charts in camping-equipment catalogues, it may appear that one stove is better than another because it takes less time to boil a quart of water or it burns less fuel in an hour, but unless your white-gas stove has the ability to run with a low, low flame you will, in fact, use much more fuel out in the field if you're doing any cooking more civilized than boiling water. It's a hassle to start stoves again and again, and always we seem to end up letting them run while preparing the next thing to put on the flame, so its nice to be able to turn the stove way down while you're getting organized or while you're waiting dinner for people out fishing.

Cooking on a backpacking stove is not like cooking at home on the range. Experienced home cooks know that assembling the ingredients and having a clear preparation plan is essential to produce a good meal with everything ready to eat at the same time. This is even more important for camp cooks. Have a game plan for dinner fixed in your mind and dinner preparation will go more smoothly from start to finish, and it will help save fuel, too. Delegate cooking jobs; don't hesitate to get others to help. While you manage the stoves, get people to cut vegetables, fetch ingredients, or wash out pots you need to use again.

And finally, a technique that saves fuel, food, and tempers, too: When you cook in a frying pan on your tiny one-burner stove, don't attempt to balance the pan on the burner, but *keep your hand on the handle constantly.* If you fail to do this, you will inevitably dump your dinner in the dirt.

Cooking at Altitude

If you cook at 8000' or higher, you'll notice that everything takes longer to cook. Water boils at a lower temperature when atmospheric pressure is lower. Water doesn't have to reach the sea-level boiling point of 212 degrees before it begins to bubble; water boils at 196.9 at 8000' and at 194 degrees at 10,000'. At 14,000', water boils at only 187.3 degrees.

How do these facts affect specific foods? Commercial dry pasta, for example, requires very hot boiling water to cook well. I've had good luck cooking thinner pastas (Angel hair, vermicelli) up to 10,000 by using furiously boiling water and a high water-to-pasta ratio, and cooking it longer. But somewhere around 11,000'—I'm not sure just where the failure line is—the water boils furiously and the pasta slowly but surely turns into a glutinous mass. I can remember cooking up a pot of something like wallpaper paste at an 11,000' camp near Mt. Lyell in Yosemite.

Bulgur wheat, instant couscous, and instant polenta cook well at 11-12,000', and regular white rice turns out great when cooked for 30 minutes at 10,000'.

I've turned out excellent biscuits, coffeecake, and cornbread in the Banks Frybake Pan up to 10,000'. Bread cookbooks tell us that at high altitude you need to decrease baking powder and other leavening agents, decrease sugar, and increase liquid, flour, and baking temperature. I've noticed that it's necessary only to increase liquids and temperature or cooking time. Oil or butter the baking pan well, because cakes and breads stick more at high altitude, too.

The steaming method of baking still works at 9500', but my cornbread takes about 45 minutes to cook. Since this method of baking depends solely on the temperature of the boiling point of water, it won't work at very high altitude where water boils at lower temperatures.

A quick and easy menu featuring plenty of liquids and carbohydrates is the answer for high-altitude cooking. For information about "Altitude, Dehydration and Your Appetite," see *Chapter 2, Good Nutrition, Good Food and the Backpacker's Appetite.*

Baking on a Backpacking Stove

There are two methods for baking on the trail, the mini-oven method and the steaming method. The mini-oven method can bake anything from *Eggplant Parmesan* to biscuits and brownies. The steaming method uses boiling-water temperatures to bake breads. For details on equipment for baking on the trail see page 69.

Mini-Oven Method

This baking method can give you results like a real oven. You need a 2-inch-deep frying pan with a snug-fitting, high lid. I use the Banks Frybake Pan, which is designed for this baking method. Simply put batter, biscuits, or casserole in the well-oiled

The Banks Frybake Pan is best for the mini-oven method of baking

pan, build a twig fire on the lid, and turn the stove down to simmer. Build up the little fire on top till you get coals, then let it bake till done, adding sticks to keep the fire hot if necessary. The trick is to keep most of the heat coming from the top and to keep the fire down below on simmer. If you don't have a stove that you can set on simmer, you'll have to use a heat diffuser (and you still may burn things on the bottom). Check food by lifting the lid, coals and all, with a pot grabber or hot pads.

This baking system is faster and uses far less cooking fuel than the steaming method. However, the mini-oven can't be used where there is no wood (above treeline) or where open fires are banned, even though it uses almost no wood at all.

Steaming Method

For baking with boiling-water temperatures you can use the BakePacker aluminum ring, which cooks your bread in a plastic bag or put together your own steaming system.

For your own steaming system, you'll need two nesting pots. To steam bread, oil the smaller pot, put in batter, and seal tightly. Make a lid of aluminum foil if the lid for the pot doesn't seal tightly, otherwise you'll get water dripping onto the dough, and a soggy bread.

Place the smaller pot inside the larger pot. Add water to the larger pot until the water surface is a couple of inches below the lip of the smaller pot. If you're using thin pots, use a metal plate or crumpled aluminum foil to separate them at the bottom. Bring water to a boil and keep boiling steadily for the recommended baking time; be sure the water doesn't boil away.

You won't get a crisp brown crust with this method, but you're not liable to overbake either. This system turns out moist and delicious quickbreads, but doesn't work well for casseroles or baked goods requiring higher cooking temperatures or long cooking times. Also, doubling a recipe results in a waste of fuel, because it takes forever to cook all the way through.

The steaming method of baking on the trail

8

Home-Drying Food

Drying food at home for your backpacking trips requires no special processing, and home-dried food is nutritious, lightweight, compact, nonperishable—and delicious. Everyone knows about things like dried fruit and jerky, but people on my trips have been amazed to learn that the spaghetti sauce they're enjoying for dinner was rehydrated from a sauce I had cooked and dried at home. Equally impressive are *Cajun Black Beans and Rice* (page 208) and *French Onion Fettucini* (page 194). All these meals can be cooked and dried at home into a lightweight, non-perishable, compact form and then reconstituted and served in camp in about 15 minutes. You can make delicious instant soups, and your home-dried fruit will taste even better than high quality health-food store products.

Carrying dried food means your pack will weigh far less: dried food is only one-third to one-twelfth the volume of the original fresh food. Fresh vegetables weigh 4 to 10 times as much as dehydrated vegetables, and fresh fruits weigh 3 to 6 times as much as the dried product. A pound of carrots, for example, dehydrates to a compact 2 ounce package and a pound of round steak becomes 6 ounces of tasty jerky. Two cups of *Cajun Black Beans* weigh 1 pound 4 ounces before being dehydrated; the dried beans weigh 8 ounces.

Dried food is nutritious. Although the drying process substantially reduces size and weight, for most foods the nutritional value is about the same as the same food frozen.

You'll save money too. Many people buy expensive freeze-dried food for their backpacking trips, but your own home-dried food will cost less and taste better. Freeze-dried food does have its place, however. See page 15 for more information on freeze-dried food.

Commercially dehydrated foods aren't as expensive as freeze-dried, but still cost 3 to 15 times more than food you dry at home. Dried apricots cost about $2 a pound to dry at home but are $8 a pound at the supermarket, and store-bought jerky costs at least four times as much as home-made jerky. Your own dehydrated food will be the lowest in price yet the highest in quality, and you'll know how it was prepared and where it came from.

If you're home-drying food for your backpacking trips to save money, you'll be well-rewarded. And if you like to cook, you'll have fun drying food. You can experiment with drying special varieties of fruits and vegetables, and dehydrate your favorite recipe for chili beans.

Here's how to get started.

Drying Food In an Oven

To dry food in your oven all you need are an accurate oven thermometer and drying racks such as a cake cooling rack or a screen. For drying pastes like spaghetti sauce use a cookie sheet with a non-stick surface.

First make sure your oven can maintain the low temperatures required for safely drying food, 130 to 150 degrees. Place your oven thermometer on the middle rack of the oven toward the back. Turn the oven on low, prop the door open 2 to 4 inches (always open the oven door a bit while drying food so moisture can escape), and check the temperature after an hour. Some ovens won't go any lower than 200 to 250 degrees and that is too high to dry most foods safely. If the temperature is too high, the food will *case harden*, which means it develops a hard shell that traps moisture inside and can cause spoilage.

If your oven can maintain 130 to 150 degrees, you're ready to start. Simply arrange the food on your drying racks in a single layer without overlapping and set in the oven for a few hours. You'll need to rotate the drying racks and remove food as it becomes dry, and you should check the temperature every 15 minutes or so until you know what your oven can do.

Drying in a Food Dehydrator

I was content to dry food in the oven until I was given a food dehydrator—what a difference! A dehydrator is much easier to use and it turns out a better product, especially with produce that has a high moisture content. My dehydrator is the Harvest Maid. I have the round model, which costs around $80 and comes with four stackable trays plus a plastic sheet for drying things like spaghetti sauce and a plastic screen for drying small or very sticky food. You can use this model with up to 12 trays, and the extra trays run about $10 each.

Food dehydrators have a thermostat that reliably keeps your food at a constant low heat, and a fan, which means that food dries much faster—two to three times faster than in an oven. A dehydrator uses less energy than an oven, and it uses less of *your* energy, too, because less time and attention are spent checking on food. Oven drying works, but if you really get into home-drying, a dehydrator is the way to go.

Making High-Quality Dried Food

You'll get high-quality results by paying attention to details. Here's how to get the most out of the time and effort you put into home drying.

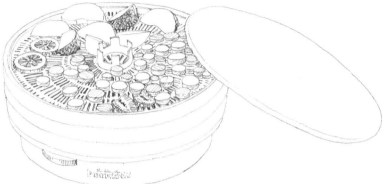

A Harvest Maid food dehydrator

Use Fresh Fruits and Vegetables at Peak Flavor

You'll get delicious results when you use high-quality food. Although it might seem that you can use any old produce, since you're going to dry the dickens out of it anyway, the fact is that starting with the best tasting fresh product gives you the best-tasting dry product. Allow fruits to ripen and sweeten, and use fresh vegetables at their peak flavor. You'll easily be able to tell the difference between dried vegetables that came from a home vegetable garden and the same kind of dried vegetables that came from the supermarket. Also, certain varieties of fruits and vegetables are more suitable for drying than others. Crisp Granny Smith and Gravenstein apples, for example, are superior to the mealier Red and Golden Delicious varieties.

Pretreat Vegetables

There are many kinds of pretreatment processes for dehydrated food—sulfuring, ascorbic acid dips, syrup blanching, and others. Partly cooking vegetables is the only pretreatment that I think is necessary for home-dried food for camping and backpacking. This cooking pretreatment of your vegetables after you cut them but before you dry them means that out on the trail they'll taste fresher, rehydrate quickly and thoroughly, and cook faster—therefore requiring less fuel.

If you don't pre-cook your home-dried veggies
they can become tough and flavorless a few weeks
after drying. This is because of continued *enzyme
action*. Enzymes are chemicals present in all fruits
and vegetables that cause them to ripen. Enzyme
action in fruits is counteracted by their higher acidity and sugar content, so it's not necessary to pre-
cook fruits before drying. However, enzymes
continue to react in most vegetables.

For example, I dried a batch of raw eggplant one
August and a week later rehydrated some of it. It
cooked perfectly well in our camp in the mountains
at 10,000'. In October—two months later—I took
more eggplant from this same batch on a backpacking trip to the Mendocino coast. It was leathery, it
resisted rehydration, and even at sea level it took
much longer to cook. I haven't had this problem
with eggplant (or any other vegetables) that I've
cooked before drying.

A microwave oven is perfect for pretreating vegetables. You don't have to use any water so a minimum of nutrients are lost, and it takes only a couple
of minutes to bring vegetables to the desired done-
ness, or I should say *underdoneness*: Your vegetables
should be slightly underdone and a bit crunchy, the
Oriental stir-fry style. If you don't have a microwave the next-best method is steaming (knowl-
edgeable cooks call this method *steam blanching*).
Note: Don't overcook. If you do your vegetables
will be mushy when reconstituted.

Not all vegetables, if uncooked, will turn tough and
leathery after a short time. Zucchini and bell peppers don't need precooking to stop enzyme action,
but I recommend it anyway. Partly cooking vegetables shortens drying time and improves color. In
camp, precooked veggies rehydrate more readily,
and when reconstituted they'll already be partly
cooked, which will save you time and fuel.

Preparing Food for the Dryer

Cut out all bruises and bad spots and peel if you wish; I usually leave peelings on. Slice, dice or grate produce; *cut into uniform pieces.* A food processor makes thin, uniform slices and is wonderful for grating. Produce about ¼ inch thick dries nicely in most cases, while over ½ inch is usually too thick. Smaller pieces of food rehydrate and cook faster.

Arrange the food on the drying racks in a single layer without overlapping, so that air can circulate freely and carry off moisture. The food will shrink considerably but you'll get even drying and superior results if you don't crowd food together.

Use the Right Temperature

Preheat your oven or dehydrator. You may use a slightly higher temperature at first, but don't forget to lower the temperature after the first couple of hours. If you're drying in an oven that doesn't maintain a low temperature, you may have to dry everything at the same temperature—this is one reason why you get a higher quality product from a dehydrator.

There are no absolutes in food drying temperatures, but here are guidelines that should help you get the best possible results. **Herbs** need to dry at low temperatures, 90 to 100 degrees. In fact, I prefer to air dry herbs in my kitchen over a period of several days. You'll probably get the best results drying **fruits** and **vegetables** at around 110 to 125 degrees. You can dry both fruits and vegetables at higher temperatures, from 125 to 145 degrees, but using a lower temperature for fruits and vegetables most often means that even though they take a little longer to dry you will get a better looking, better tasting, more nutritious product. **Meat** and **cooked main dishes** *must* be dried at 140 to 160 degrees for the first two or three hours in order to stop the growth of harmful bacteria, then the temperature can be reduced to about 130 degrees.

Don't Just Time Food— Watch It

The time needed to dry different foods varies by hours and depends on many factors: ripeness, moisture content, thickness of pieces, size of the load in the dryer, temperature, altitude, humidity, and so on. You cannot simply set a timer and leave food to dry. To get high-quality results you must check the food to see how quickly it's drying.

Nevertheless, it's good to have a general idea of how long it takes certain foods to dry. Herbs dry relatively quickly, sometimes in only an hour or two. Vegetables are in the middle, taking anywhere from 3 to 8 hours. Spaghetti sauce and soup base pastes take around 8 hours. Thinly sliced beef jerky needs only 6 to 8 hours. Cooked beans dry surprisingly fast, in only 4 to 6 hours. Fruit takes longest, usually 8 to 12 hours with some things like apricot halves taking up to 24 hours, and it takes 24 to 36 hours to turn grapes into raisins.

Don't Dry Food Too Long

Drying food too long is probably the most common mistake made. Remember that food may appear to need more drying time when actually it is merely soft and pliable from the heat of the dryer. Take food out of your dryer a bit *before* you think it's ready and let it cool. You may find that most of it is ready. Sort out pieces that are too moist and put them back in to finish drying. Also note that the drying process can seem to take forever, but once food gets to the point where it's *almost* ready, drying progresses quickly and food can become too dry before you know it.

Although checking food is more important than timing, it helps to know how long it's been drying. Each time I put something in the dryer I note the time on a self-sticking note and stick it on top of the dehydrator. The note reminds me when to pay close attention, and it's handy for keeping records later, too.

Finally, I recommend that you never leave food drying for hours on end without checking it. Almost every time I have done this, it turns out to be too dry. It's a great disappointment to find that the luscious ripe fruit you started with has become tough, brittle, and practically inedible. If you're not able to check drying food for several hours, just switch off the oven or dehydrator and start it again when you can check on it often.

Testing for Dryness

Taste and touch are the best way to tell when food is optimally dry. Take the food you're testing out of the dryer and let it cool. Herbs and leafy things crumble when they are completely dry. Dried fruit is leathery and pliable—taste it, it can be somewhat moist. It's all right for fruit to retain 15 to 20% of its moisture, because its high sugar and acid content help prevent spoilage. Dried vegetables are relatively brittle—they lose 95% of their moisture. Jerky is dry enough if it cracks when you bend it, but not so brittle that it breaks. Cooked main dishes such as spaghetti sauce can be bendable but should have no sign of moisture.

Freshly Dried Food Tastes Best

Drying has traditionally been a way to preserve food. In the summertime our ancestors dried food that they would not be able to obtain in the winter, and when most of us think about dried food we think of it as a way to keep food for many months. Yet most backpackers and campers are interested in drying food to make it lightweight and to keep it nonperishable for only a few weeks at most.

I've found that if used within a short time after dehydration, home-dried food is so delicious that it's difficult to tell whether it's fresh or dried. I will often dry food on a Monday that I serve to my backpacking group the following Saturday, and it tastes like fresh food. Most people can't tell the difference.

You can dry most foods months ahead of time, but if you want optimum flavor from your home-dried food I recommend drying it only a few weeks before your trip at most. Dried fruit stays delicious for many months, but vegetables taste best when eaten within a few weeks.

To guard against the dangers of spoilage, I recommend that you do not use precooked main dishes and soups more than two or three weeks after they've been dried and that you store them in the refrigerator. They're at peak flavor for only a few weeks anyway.

In general, most home-dried food keeps safely for six months to one year, but be aware that dried food loses both flavor and nutritional value over time.

Storing Dried Food

Store dried food in a dark, cool place. I keep all my dehydrated food in the refrigerator. You can store dried food at room temperature, but temperatures below 60 degrees keep it fresher, better tasting, and more nutritious.

Packaging Dried Food

Wait until food is completely cool before packaging. Protect it from moisture by storing in plastic ziploc bags with the extra air squeezed out. If you have a home vacuum-packaging machine or a bag sealer such as Seal-A-Meal, which use boilable plastic bags, these are excellent ways to store your dehydrated food and you can rehydrate food right in these boilable plastic bags. If you have a good vacuum-packaging machine it will make a big difference in the length of time your dried food stays fresh.

Keep checking your food for a couple of weeks after you've dried it. If it hasn't dried long enough, you'll see moisture, but the food can usually be saved if you simply put it back in the dryer.

Package everything in usable quantities. You may find it's most efficient to package consistent amounts too. For example, I package all main dishes in 4-cup (before drying) quantities.

Labeling Dried Food

Label everything. Always write down the date and say what the food is; several weeks later you might be surprised to find you have no idea what this "green stuff" is.

Note the weight if you have a food scale, but even more important say what the fresh equivalent was: "2 oz carrots. Was 2 large carrots when fresh." Stating the fresh equivalent will help you figure the right amount of food to pack. Dried food becomes so light and compact that we tend to bring too much.

Write down what you had in mind for the food when you dried it: "Mixed veggies. Use for minestrone or pilaf." Or make special notes: "6 oz Black Beans, was 4 cups before drying. Don't add too much rehydrating water or you'll have bean soup." Or: "2 oz Onion Soup Base. Add 1 beef bouillon cube for best flavor." Sentimental stuff is nice, too: "Watermelon. With help from Matt & Mike," or "Dad's Special Winesaps."

Keeping Records

Your records will remind you of good food you want to use again, and of new things you want to try, and will keep you from making the same mistake twice.

I devised a simple form for my food drying records, and keep them in a three-ring binder. Each time I dry something, I fill in the date, length of time dried, size of the pieces, and so on. Later I make notes on how the food was used, and how it could be better, and I perhaps include a recipe. Your records don't have to be this elaborate. You can simply put the relevant information on the label with some space for comments like "Great" or "Not so hot," bring it home from your trip and toss it in a manila folder, plastic bag and all.

Rehydrating Food on the Trail

To rehydrate dried food, simply pour water over the food to cover and set aside for 15 to 30 minutes or until the food has absorbed water. Here are some tips for getting the best results when you rehydrate food on the trail:

- Use boiling water to rehydrate food in the shortest time. Cold water doesn't work well.

- Put the lid on the pot to trap steam and warmth. If you're rehydrating food in the boilable plastic bag it's packaged in, twist the bag closed—and make sure it's set between rocks or on something solid so that it won't collapse and spill. To keep it warm even longer and speed rehydration, insulate with a jacket or other clothing.

- Most foods take 15 to 30 minutes to rehydrate, and seem to do better rehydrating quietly and slowly. Dried vegetables thrown into a pot of furiously boiling water for 10 minutes are likely to be tougher than they would be if you brought them around gently.

- A longer rehydrating time means that your food will be more tender, and that it will take less time and less fuel to cook it. If you get into camp early in the day, start rehydrating dinner in the afternoon.

- The rehydrating water is full of flavor and nutrients, so use it in your recipe—or drink it. The water from carrots and fruits is delicious.

- When reconstituting foods like spaghetti sauce, be careful not to add too much water or you'll end up with a thin, soupy sauce. When rehydrating fruits and vegetables, add just enough water to cover so the hydrating water will be concentrated for using in your recipe. You can always add more water if necessary.

- If you're rehydrating something like eggplant that soaks up lots of water, it will cook better if you gently squeeze out the excess water before cooking—particularly if you're going to stir-fry or sauté it.

Foods to Home-dry For Backpacking

In this section I've noted which fruits and vegetables I've had especially good results home-drying for camping trips. Apples, apricots, cherries, figs, papaya, pears (one of my favorites), plums, peaches, and nectarines are delicious dried. Dehydrated strawberries are excellent for dessert sauces and trail snacks. Your home-dried pineapple will be much tastier than the sugar-laden stuff sold commercially; dry it at a low temperature, 100 to 110 degrees. Citrus should be dried at a low temperature, too. Try dehydrating orange, lime or lemon rounds—you can add them to flavor stewed dried fruit or as a garnish in good old mountain stream water. Dehydrated watermelon tastes like watermelon taffy. Home-dried raisins are outstanding; try drying muscat grapes. Bananas cut in quarters lengthwise and dried till pliable and moist are a great favorite.

Almost any variety of peppers takes well to home drying: pasilla, Anaheim, pimiento, sweet red, yellow, and green bell peppers. Rehydrated shredded carrots and cabbage make crisp refreshing salads, or try the recipe for *Alsatian Cabbage* on page 181. Eggplant, leeks, scallions, onions, parsley, potatoes, sweet potatoes, tomatoes and zucchini are just a few of the vegetables that are great for camp meals, and you'll find many dishes using home-dried vegetables in the recipe section.

In addition to fresh fruits and vegetables you can dry cooked legumes such as lima beans, lentils, black beans and navy beans. Simply cook plain beans till done and dry for about six hours. *Minestrone, Indian Sambaar Stew,* and *Dilled Baby Lima Salad* are among the recipes in this book which use dehydrated beans. You can also make your own home-dried tomato paste by dehydrating canned tomato paste; to use, simply drop the dried sheets of tomato paste into soups or pasta sauce, and they'll quickly rehydrate.

What Foods Don't Dry Well

By now you may have some creative ideas of your own for home-dried camping food. I've found that you never can tell what will work until you try it—and I've been pleasantly *and* unpleasantly surprised at the results I've gotten. For example, I felt that dried watermelon probably wouldn't taste

very good until a couple I met on a hike told me it
was fantastic. They were right.

I've also had some bright ideas that failed. Sharing
these failures with you may save you some time.

Meat on the trail is best enjoyed as jerky. Dried
hamburger can give a meaty flavor to things like
spaghetti sauce, but it's crunchy—no matter how
long you cook it. If you expect succulent chunks of
meat in your dinner pot, you'll be disappointed.
Dried meats stay dry, and that's how they should
be eaten. They don't rehydrate well and don't taste
particularly good rehydrated, either. Chicken has
the texture of cardboard, tuna becomes overbear-
ingly fishy, beef is tough and stringy. If you feel a
need for meat, chicken, or fish as a main dish after
several days in the backcountry, you'd best make
do with canned chicken and tuna, commercial dry
sausages containing salt and other preservatives—
or settle for freeze-dried meat. Better yet, go fishing.

Home-dried tofu is not a winner, either. If taste is
your standard, your best bet for tofu on the trail is
the unrefrigerated vacuum-packed kind. See the
glossary for more details on tofu.

Dehydrated lettuce is crackly and dry, a lost cause.
Cucumbers and radishes are borderline. They actually do impart their flavors to a salad, but the texture leaves too much to be desired. Give it a try only
if you're a real salad hound.

Dried cilantro isn't worth bothering with. When
fresh, this herb adds sparkle and wonderful flavor
to dishes. When dried, it loses practically all its
flavor and there's no point in using it.

I tried making my own quick-cooking grains and
experimented with barley and brown rice. I cooked
them thoroughly before drying, then rehydrated
and cooked them in camp. It works, but takes almost as long as cooking the grains from scratch,
and isn't worth the trouble. Moreover, you can find

plenty of good commercial instant grains. Arrowhead Mills makes an excellent quick brown rice
that cooks in 12 minutes.

And finally, you should not attempt to home-dry
eggs, milk and milk products because of the high
risk of food poisoning. Commercially dried dairy
products are processed rapidly at high temperatures using methods that can't be duplicated with
your home dryer. Milkman is an excellent choice
for dehydrated milk, and you can carry eggs fresh,
commercially dried or freeze-dried.

9

Introduction to the Recipes

The recipes in this book are for people who like to eat well in the backcountry. Many are easy to prepare, a few are for more dedicated cooks. Because the way you pack the food for your camping or backpacking trip goes hand in hand with these recipes, I highly recommend you read *Chapter 5 Packing Food and Keeping It Fresh.*

In most cases, the first item listed in a recipe is preferable. If the recipe says, for example, add ½ cup leeks or ¼ cup onions—the leeks would make it taste better, but onions are fine, too.

Dehydrated vs. Fresh Foods

In any of the recipes that call for dehydrated foods you can substitute freeze-dried or fresh food. See page 83 for information on how to rehydrate dried food.

For good taste, fresh foods are almost always preferable. But in the interests of light weight and avoiding spoilage, you can tailor these recipes to when you'll eat the meal. For example, the *Eggplant Parmesan* recipe on page 189, if made at the beginning of a short trip where weight is not a big issue, might be made from a can of whole tomatoes, fresh parsley, Mozzarella and Parmesan cheese. For *Eggplant Parmesan* later in the trip you could use tomato flakes and sun-dried tomatoes, dried parsley, and just Parmesan cheese.

And it's worth repeating that fresh meat and dishes made with eggs and cream will quickly spoil if they are not kept chilled. The recipes in this book using these ingredients are meant to be eaten the first night if you can't keep them cold.

Many of the dishes in my recipes will taste better if simmered longer. Some are ready to eat in 15 minutes, but their flavor will be greatly improved if the flavors are allowed to mingle for another 30 minutes. This doesn't mean that the dish has to stay on the stove using up precious fuel. You can set it aside in a warm place while you set up camp or go fishing and then reheat it when you're ready to eat. Some dishes, like pasta, ought to be eaten as soon as they're cooked, and the recipe will say so.

Butter

Real butter, fresh garlic, and fresh onions are called for in many of the recipes in this book. I think these three ingredients are essential to good cooking.

Real butter has gotten a bad reputation in recent years. People seem to think that margarine is somehow healthier when in fact it has just as many calories as butter. You can substitute margarine for butter in the recipes, but unless you're fighting a serious cholesterol problem, I don't know why you'd want to. Used in cooking, butter adds a richness to food that margarine cannot possibly impart, and only a small amount of butter is necessary to confer this incomparable flavor.

Moreover, butter does a fantastic job of masking (or at least improving) the taste of some foods we backpackers must necessarily use such as powdered milk, powdered eggs, and dehydrated vegetables. As noted in *Chapter 5*, salted butter instead of sweet butter is recommended for backpacking because it keeps longer.

I should add that I don't recommend eating butter to this extent in your diet at home (I never spread it on bread), but I think that it's important for back-packers carrying a pack for miles on end and possibly being exposed to cold weather conditions to get a ration of oil, and indulging in butter only as often as you go backpacking is not likely to be harmful to your health. Reduce the amount of butter in the recipes if you wish. If you insist on cutting it out all together, I think the best substitute (except in baking sweets) is olive oil, not margarine.

Onions and Garlic

A fresh onion keeps well, and—except on long trips—I think an onion makes up for its extra weight in the great flavor it gives to foods. As the French say, "Onions marry the flavors."

Fresh garlic weighs next to nothing, and the taste of fresh garlic is incomparably better than garlic powder or granules. I don't care for the taste of dried onions or garlic granules or powder. To me, there's a distinct processed taste to foods that contain dried onions and garlic.

Nevertheless, if you're committed to no-fuss cooking or the lightest pack possible, then substitute dried onions and garlic for fresh. Approximately ⅛ teaspoon of garlic powder or ¼ teaspoon of garlic granules equal 1 clove of garlic. Two tablespoons of onion flakes or 1 tablespoon of onion powder equals about 4 tablespoons of fresh onion.

Sautéeing onions, garlic, and spices in oil before adding other ingredients to a recipe always makes a dish taste better. In the recipes here you usually can combine all ingredients together at once without disastrous results, but you'll get far better results if the dish is cooked according to recipe directions.

Alcohol

Many of my recipes call for a shot of wine or spirits. Liquor adds a subtle, rich dimension to food, and the alcohol quickly evaporates in cooking, but if you object to alcohol leave it out of the recipe.

Dry Milk	I *highly* recommend Milkman brand powdered milk. Milkman tastes far better than any other brand I've tried, but if it isn't available in your area use any dry milk. One cup of powdered Milkman makes one quart of milk; if you're using another brand you may need to change the recipe accordingly.
Eggs	The recipes that contain powdered eggs have, instead of a whole egg, ¼ cup powdered egg plus ¼ cup water, and the water has been factored into the recipe. If you use a powdered-egg mix that doesn't fit this formula, adjust the recipe accordingly.
Wheat Gluten	Wheat gluten is called for in many of the bread recipes. Wheat gluten is the natural protein derived from wheat, and is used to produce consistent, uniform breads. You can omit the gluten, but it will improve breads containing bran, nuts, raisins, seeds or non-wheat flours. It makes breads taste better and adds to the protein value, too.
Salt	It's usually best to wait and taste before you add any salt in cooking. You may be using products that have more salt than you expect. Recipes using several canned products or soy sauce or bouillon cubes may turn out to be too salty. Buy low-salt products and don't add salt until you've added all ingredients and tasted.
Bouillon Cubes	Salt is the first ingredient in most brands of bouillon cubes, and they usually contain MSG, too. You may omit bouillon cubes from any recipe or substitute health-food-store unsalted, non-MSG bouillon powder (but you may not care for its rather yeasty taste). You might think adding a few extra beef or chicken bouillon cubes would make a dish taste richer, but not so. It just tastes bad.
Adding Spices	Go light when adding spices, add gradually, and taste as you go. Inexperienced cooks can ruin an entire meal with heavy-handed use of spices. Just a little tarragon, for example, can make a delicious

omelette—but if you use too much tarragon you will have an inedible omelette. Use fresh herbs whenever you can—they have a better flavor than dried herbs.

And finally, be adventurous with your cooking. If you can't find an ingredient, try substituting something else. Buy vegetables you've never heard of. Unleash your curiosity and don't hesitate to experiment. In any recipe, add ingredients to your own taste. Cut loose, be creative, and have a good time cooking.

10

Breakfasts

Although it's arguable that "breakfast is the most important meal of the day," even people who never eat breakfast find that they need to eat before shouldering a backpack and hiking down the trail, and nutritionists tell us that proteins are best utilized when eaten at breakfast.

Breakfast in the wilderness can be a late and leisurely affair, but more often it must accommodate an early start. Most of the breakfasts here will get you moving early and keep you going. A few are for slow mornings when you have time to sip your coffee and watch the sun slanting through the trees.

Cowboy Coffee

Purists may bring their tidy paper coffee filters, but campers who are into the romance of roughing it prefer to add coffee grounds directly to the water. Coffee made this way is affectionately known as hobo, or cowboy, coffee. Some people claim that sprinkling cold water into the freshly brewed coffee settles the grounds.

Boiling water
A high-quality, regular-grind coffee: 2 TB of coffee for each cup and 2 TB for the pot (for 4 or more servings)

In Camp: Bring water to a boil. Stir in coffee and keep stirring for about 30 seconds to a minute and remove from heat. Cover pot and let steep in a warm place for 5 to 10 minutes, depending on how strong you want the brew. Pour into cups through a tea strainer.

Cereals

Cereal is quick and easy and sticks to your ribs when served with milk and butter. Most supermarket instant packaged cereals are not terribly nourishing, and they taste rather empty, but some excellent quick cereals can be found in health-food-stores; Erehwon and Arrowhead Mills are good brands.

Bulgur, instant polenta, couscous, quick brown rice, and kasha all make hearty, fast breakfasts, and you can fortify any cereal by adding things like sunflower seeds, wheat germ, and dried fruit. Good old granola can be a hot or a cold cereal.

Tip: To keep milk powder from lumping in your hot cereal, put granola or other dry cereal in your cup with a couple of tablespoons of dry milk and mix together, then add hot water. You'll have a steaming hot cup of cereal with no lumps.

Summit Breakfast

Makes 4 servings

I always serve this fast and filling breakfast the morning we climb to the summit of Mt. Whitney.

1 cup whole wheat instant couscous
½-1 cup Medjool or other dates
Optional: milk, butter, brown sugar

At Home:

Package dates and couscous in separate plastic bags.

In Camp:

1. Combine dates and 1¾ cup water in a pot and bring to a boil. **2.** Stir couscous into boiling water, cover and remove from heat. Set in a warm place for 5 minutes, slightly longer at high elevations. **3.** Serve with milk, butter, and/or brown sugar if you wish.

House of the Sun Bulgur

Makes 4 servings

This hiker's breakfast came about one morning when my friend Lane and I combined the last of our food before walking out of the Haleakala crater on Maui.

1 cup bulgur
A mixture of 1 cup of dried, chopped fruit such as:
    papaya
    pineapple
    apricots
    mangoes
    bananas
1 TB chopped candied ginger
¼ cup chopped macadamia nuts *or* walnuts

At Home: Pack dried fruits, ginger and nuts together. Pack bulgur in a plastic bag.

In Camp: 1. Add fruits, ginger and nuts to 2 cups of water and bring to a boil. 2. Stir in bulgur, cover, and cook over low heat for about 15 minutes. On days when we need to get an early start, I make this cereal the night before, and package it in individual ziplocs, and people eat it on the trail.

Piute Polenta

Makes 4 servings

1 cup instant polenta
2-4 TB pine nuts
⅓ cup raisins
Optional: milk, butter, honey or brown sugar
butter

At Home: Package polenta in a plastic bag. Put pine nuts and raisins together in a plastic bag. Add milk, butter, honey or brown sugar, and butter to main supply.

In Camp: 1. Bring 1¾ cups water to a boil with pine nuts and raisins. 2. Stir in polenta and cook until thick, this will take just a couple of minutes. 3. Cover and remove from heat for 5 minutes. Stir in milk, butter, and honey or brown sugar and serve.

Fried Polenta and Sausages

Makes 4 servings

Fried polenta is great just by itself, and extra good cooked with sausages. You can use health-food-store soy sausages, or fancy deli sausages such as chicken apple, or try it with the next recipe Turkey Sage Sausage.

1 cup instant polenta
4 oz or more of sausages, sliced, whole or patties
safflower oil

At Home: Package polenta in a plastic bag. Put sausages in a brown paper bag. Add oil to main supply.

In Camp: 1. Either the night before or about an hour before breakfast, cook polenta in boiling water as directed. Pour into a lightly-oiled shallow pan such as a frying pan and allow to cool. When polenta has set, cut bars about 2" x 4". Set aside. 2. Cook sausage in frying pan. Add a little extra oil to pan juices. Heat oil and fry polenta over medium heat. Fry until a transparent crust forms on one side, then turn and do the other side. Serve hot.

Turkey Sage Sausage

Makes 6-8 servings

This sausage will be fine for breakfast the first morning of your trip if you freeze it and keep it chilled until you start hiking, but fresh meat is not safe to eat if you can't keep it chilled.

2 lbs ground turkey
½ tsp salt
1 tsp fresh ground pepper
1 TB crushed sage
Optional: ¼ tsp cayenne

At Home: 1. In a large mixing bowl combine all ingredients. 2. Shape into 4" patties, wrap with a layer of wax paper between patties and freeze.

In Camp: Cook thawed patties in frying pan over medium-high heat.

Hash Brown Sweet Potatoes
With Cilantro Pesto

Makes 6 servings

2-4 TB safflower oil
4-6 sweet potatoes, baked, sliced lengthwise, and
    cut in ¼" hunks *or* **1½ cups grated, cooked, and**
    dehydrated sweet potatoes
1 small onion, cut in rings
salt and pepper
***Cilantro-Peanut Oil Pesto* (page 179)**

At Home:
Package oil with main supply. Bake potatoes and cool, pack whole potatoes in brown paper bags or if you're using dehydrated sweet potatoes, package them in a ziploc or boilable plastic bag. Pack onion in brown paper bag. Make *Cilantro-Peanut Pesto Oil* and put in nalgene bottle.

In Camp:
1. If you're using dried potatoes, rehydrate. When rehydrated, drain and pat excess moisture out with a cloth. If you're using baked potatoes, slice as directed above. 2. Sauté onion in oil. Add potatoes and cook over medium-high heat until brown and crusty, about 15 minutes. (Dehydrated potatoes can take longer to cook than most dehydrated foods.) 3. Spoon a couple of tablespoons of pesto over potatoes before serving.

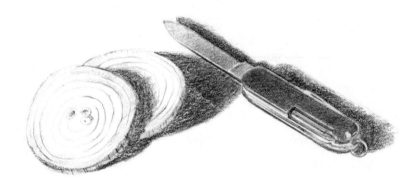

Bill's Trout

My father has been trout fishing in the Sierra for sixty years. This how he cooks up a mess of trout for breakfast. Serve with pancakes, bacon and fried eggs. If you object to bacon, use a vegetable oil to cook your trout.

fresh trout
Dredge in:
    equal parts of white flour and cornmeal, salt and pepper to taste
Fry in:
    bacon drippings

At Home: Combine dredging flours and salt and pepper in a large ziploc. Bring some bacon to make drippings or bring drippings from home in a wide-mouth nalgene jar.

In Camp: **1.** Clean fish soon after they're caught. Keep in cool place until ready to cook. **2.** Dredge trout in flour mixture. Melt 2-4 TB bacon drippings in a frying pan. Lay trout in pan and cook over medium heat for just a few minutes, depending on size. They tend to curl up when freshly caught, so use a pancake turner to gently flatten them so they'll brown all over. Don't worry if some of them fall apart— they do that when fresh, too. When they have a nice brown crust on the skin and the flesh is no longer translucent and flakes with a bit of pressure, they're done.

Frying Pan Toast

Here's the easiest way to make toast in camp: No need to hold bread on a stick over a fire—simply put it in a frying pan and toast over medium-high heat, with butter or not. Spread with honey or jam or thick stewed fruit.

For cinnamon toast, butter well and sprinkle sugar and cinnamon over the melted butter. To make milktoast, pour warm milk over the crusty, warm cinnamon toast.

Scottish Prunes
Makes 4-6 servings

A breakfast to get you moving in the morning. Put over hot cereal or pancakes.

1 cup pitted prunes
1 fresh lemon, sliced in rounds *or* **4-6 dehydrated lemon rounds**

At Home: Package prunes in ziploc. Put whole lemon or dehydrated lemon slices in brown paper bag.

In Camp: **1.** Put prunes in a cooking pot and cover with an inch of boiling water. **2.** Slice fresh lemon and add to prunes or add dehydrated lemon to prunes and cover. **3.** Prunes are ready in a couple of hours, but are best if they sit overnight. Because they're high in sugar, they'll keep for a few days if kept cool.

Pancakes

Pancakes are not ideal for early starts. They're better suited for those days when breakfast is called brunch.

To mix batter, stir just enough to moisten. Batter will thicken as it sits and can be thinned with water. I've always found it a good idea to reserve a small amount of the flour mixture in case I add too much water. To cook pancakes, heat lightly oiled frying pan over medium-high heat. Pan is hot enough when a little cold water flicked on it beads up and dances around the pan before disappearing. Pour a spoonful of batter in frying pan, and turn when bubbles form and pop. Turn pancakes only once. To make a perfect pancake over the small one-burner backpacking stove, cook only one at a time in the center of your pan. I'm not sure why, but the first one seldom turns out.

Serve pancakes with jam, *Strawberry Sauce* (page 215), or real maple syrup, or boysenberry or coconut syrup warmed in a nalgene bottle in a pan of hot water. Add freeze-dried blueberries, corn, or peas to batter. Or add rehydrated apples with a touch of cinnamon. Minced green onion and a little grated cheese are good, too. Make extra pancakes and eat for lunch. Spartans on long trips report that they rely on pancakes for their bread.

If you don't want to make your pancakes from scratch using the following recipes, most health-food-store mixes are very good. So are some imported mixes for Swedish pancakes and hearty potato pancakes.

Corn Oatcakes
Makes twelve 5-inch pancakes

½ **cup whole wheat flour**
½ **cup cornmeal**
¼ **cup oat flour**
2 TB oat bran
1 TB sugar
1 tsp baking powder
½ **tsp baking soda**
½ **tsp salt**
⅓ **cup dry milk**
½ **cup powdered egg**
¼ **cup safflower oil**
1 tsp vanilla
1½-2 cups water

At Home: Package all dry ingredients together. Combine oil and vanilla in a small nalgene bottle.

In Camp: **1.** Combine dry ingredients with oil mixture and water and mix. **2.** Cook pancakes.

Buckwheat Cakes

Makes eight 5-inch pancakes

½ cup buckwheat flour
½ cup whole wheat flour
1 tsp baking powder
½ tsp baking soda
1 TB sugar
4 TB buttermilk powder
¼ cup powdered egg
¼ cup safflower oil
1¼ cups water

At Home: Combine dry ingredients in a plastic bag. Add oil to main supply.

In Camp: 1. Combine dry ingredients with oil mixture and water and mix. 2. Cook pancakes.

Whole Wheat Pancakes With Bananas

Makes ten 6-inch pancakes

I serve banana pancakes with coconut syrup in Hawaii. If you're in Hawaii, get the tasty little apple bananas for these pancakes.

1½ cups whole wheat flour
2½ tsp baking powder
½ tsp salt
⅓ cup dry milk
3 TB safflower oil
1¼ cups water
3 bananas, sliced

At Home: Combine dry ingredients in a ziploc bag. Add oil to main supply. Put bananas in brown paper bags.

In Camp: 1. Combine dry ingredients with oil and water and mix. 2. Slice bananas and set aside; *do not stir into batter or pancakes will stick.* 3. Pour a spoonful of batter in frying pan, then lay a few banana slices on the raw dough. Turn when bubbles form in dough. The banana side will tend to stick a bit, so it helps to keep oiling pan lightly with an oil-soaked piece of paper towel.

Omelettes Omelettes taste best, of course, made with fresh eggs. But fresh eggs are awfully heavy, so backpackers often use freeze-dried or powdered eggs. Freeze-dried eggs are much more expensive than powdered eggs, but they taste much better. You can improve the taste of either freeze-dried or powdered eggs by using a little fresh sautéed green onion or garlic in your omelette, and by combining fresh and dried eggs. Only 1 or 2 fresh eggs in a 6-egg omelette will make it taste a lot better. See page 51 for tips on packing fresh eggs in your backpack.

You can combine eggs with just about anything— vegetables, rice, pesto, and salsa. A smoked salmon and chive omelette served with bagels and cream cheese makes a fine brunch. Some people think the best omelette in the world is the *Hangtown Fry*.

Hangtown Fry

Makes 4 servings

This dish originated in my home-town of Placerville, California, and today is served in many of the best restaurants in San Francisco. Placerville was called Hangtown during the days of the gold rush, and legend has it that men condemned to the hangman's noose would request a Hangtown Fry for their last meal.

6-8 slices bacon, cut in half horizontally
1 12-oz can whole oysters
flour for dredging oysters, about ½ cup
¾ cup soda cracker crumbs *or* **¾ cup bread crumbs**
8 fresh eggs *or* **freeze-dried eggs making the**
     equivalent of 8 eggs
salt and pepper
Optional: 1 green onion, minced

At Home: Package bacon in butcher paper or brown paper bag. Put onion (if used) in brown paper bag. Package flour and crumbs in separate ziploc bags. Pack fresh eggs or freeze-dried eggs and the can of oysters.

In Camp: 1. Add liquid to freeze-dried eggs according to directions or lightly beat fresh eggs and set aside. 2. Fry bacon till crisp. Remove from pan and set aside. 3. Drain oysters and discard liquid. Dredge oysters in flour, then dip in eggs, then in bread crumbs and fry in bacon drippings over medium heat until golden brown. Take care not to overcook oysters. 4. Gently drain excess bacon drippings from pan if necessary. Add eggs and half the cooked bacon to oysters and stir carefully until until eggs are cooked. When the eggs are done, put the rest of the bacon on top, sprinkle with minced green onion and serve.

Hit-the-Trail Fritatta

Makes 9 squares

I serve this already-cooked fritatta for breakfast when we've all met at the trailhead the night before and need to get an early start; leftovers make a great lunch. Since this dish is made with eggs, it will spoil after the first day unless it's kept chilled.

> ½ cup diced onion
> 1 clove garlic, minced
> ½ tsp oregano
> 1 zucchini, sliced in rounds
> 2 TB fresh basil, chopped
> 2 baked potatoes, sliced
> 3 eggs, beaten
> olive oil
> ½ cup grated Parmesan cheese
> salt and pepper

At Home: 1. Sauté onion, garlic and oregano in oil till onion is translucent. Add zucchini and basil and cook over medium-high heat for 2 minutes. 2. Remove from heat and stir in sliced baked potatoes, Parmesan, and beaten eggs. Season to taste. Pour into an oiled 8" square pan and bake at 350 degrees for 15-20 minutes. 3. Remove from heat, allow to cool, and slice into squares.

11

Lunches, Trail Snacks, and Drinks

I think the best lunch, all things considered, is leftover breakfast or dinner. Other good lunch foods are jelly and nut butters in plastic food tubes; small cans of tuna, sardines and oysters and other specialty fish; cheese (dry Jack, aged Gouda, Reggiano, and Parmesan are delicious and last a long time); cream cheese (great with chutney); celery, carrots, apples; dried fruit: dates, apricots, pears, prunes, raisins, and so on; peanut-butter-filled pretzels (they hit the spot), energy bars, pemmican bars and Kendal Mint Cake (for high-altitude climbing and hiking), and other candy bars (remember, you'll crave and use more sugar); packaged instant hummus (add water on the trail or make ahead and carry in a food tube) and already-baked potatoes (try them with Dijon mustard); breads and crackers: pilot bread, hard rye crackers, pocket bread, bagels, Westphalian pumpernickel, rice crackers, and dense, sweet breads. Vegetable pâtés and gourmet condiments such as fancy mustards carried in film cans are fun to bring along, too.

And then there's the inevitable trail mix. Trail mix *is* good trail food, but be aware that some palates can take only so much of it. People get tired of trail mix early in the trip, and I often see huge, bulging bags of it left over and carried out. My favorite trail mix is simply muscat raisins mixed with toasted, salted sunflower seeds.

In general, I favor large breakfasts and dinners, with snacks and smaller lunches along the trail. Lunch food is *heavy*, so be realistic about how much you can eat.

In addition to the recipes for lunches and trail snacks in this chapter, there are many other recipes in this book which make great lunch food. Among them are *Herbed Sun-Dried Tomatoes, Mexican Tabouli, Chinese Grain Salad, Basil Pesto, South of the Border Pesto, Jono's Herb Rolls, Mer's Prune Cake, Buckwheat Molasses Mountain Bread, Oat Date Bread, Peggy's Date Sticks, Madeline's Jam Squares,* and any of the jerky recipes in *Chapter 15*.

High-Power Peanut Butter
Makes 2 cups

These nut butter spreads have a high calorie-to-weight ratio, and the added powdered milk makes a complete protein. Spread on bread or crackers or dried fruit; this one is especially good on dried bananas.

> ¾ **cup peanut butter**
> ¼ **cup tahini**
> ½ **cup dry milk**
> ½ **cup bran cereal**
> ½ **cup honey** *or* **blackstrap molasses**
> ½ **cup currants** *or* **raisins**

At Home: Combine all ingredients and spoon into a wide-mouth nalgene jar. If you want a stiffer spread, work in more dry milk, bran or currants; for a creamier spread add more honey or a vegetable oil such as sunflower oil.

Honey-Date Cashew Butter
Makes 2 cups

1 cup cashew butter
½ cup diced dates
½ cup dry milk
¼ cup honey

At Home: Combine all ingredients and spoon into a wide-mouth nalgene jar. If you want a stiffer spread, work in more dry milk or dates; for a creamier spread add more honey or a little vegetable oil such as sunflower oil.

Orange Marmalade-Almond Butter
Makes 2 cups

1 cup almond butter
½ cup orange marmalade, more if you wish
½ cup dry milk

At Home: Combine all ingredients and spoon into a wide-mouth nalgene jar. If you want a stiffer spread, work in more dry milk; for a creamier spread add more marmalade or a vegetable oil such as sunflower oil.

JoAnne's Ginger Balls
Makes 12 servings

This is a recipe my sister always makes at Christmas time. It makes a great trail snack, too.

½ cup dried apricots
½ cup dried pineapple
¼ cup flaked and sweetened coconut
¼ cup golden raisins
½ cup dried papaya
¼ cup candied ginger
2 TB water, if necessary

At Home: Finely mince dry fruit and ginger (use a food processor if you have one). Add a little water if necessary (it depends on how much moisture there is is the dried fruit). Form into balls. Roll in powdered sugar if desired.

Drinks   Drinking plenty of liquids is necessary to feeling right when you're carrying a backpack; three or four liters a day is not too much. (For more information on purifying water see *Chapter 7*, and read about dehydration in *Chapter 2*.)

Plain water is the best drink of all, but concentrated lemonade and fruit-flavored powders may tempt you to drink more. Some people like fresh lemon slices in their hiking water, and dehydrated orange or lemon slices are good, too. Try the flavorful rehydrating water you used with apples, cherries, apricots, etc. for energizing and nutritious fruit drinks. You can also use powdered, dried vegetables like carrots or tomatoes to make juice.

Electrolyte replacement drinks are popular and some hikers like to add a teaspoon of instant tea to a quart of Gatorade. Or try this home-made formula for replenishing body salts: a quart of water mixed with ¼ teaspoon of salt and a pinch of baking soda, plus a squeeze of lemon for flavor.

Alcohol is dehydrating and may intensify the effects of high altitude. And, contrary to popular belief, alcohol will not keep you warm in cold weather, but in fact can promote hypothermia. However, if used in moderation there's nothing wrong with a relaxing cocktail after a day on the trail. Backpackers usually carry liquor in a small nalgene flask, and camp cocktails range from hot chocolate with peppermint schnapps to bourbon and branch water. Some campers are partial to Harvey's Bristol Creme Sherry and—believe it or not—Meyer's rum and Tang is really good.

Caffeine teas and coffee, although not taboo, are slightly dehydrating and should not be counted toward your daily liquid intake. There's a recipe for *Cowboy Coffee* in the **Breakfasts** chapter. Swiss Miss hot chocolate (for backpacking the one that contains real sugar instead of a sugar substitute is preferable) and powdered apple cider are favorite hot drinks.

Herb teas, hot or cold, are popular. Chamomile, mint, lemon zinger and Yogi tea are favorites on my trips. The best tea at high altitude is *Ginger Tea*.

Ginger Tea

Makes 8 cups

Although the only real "cure" for altitude sickness is acclimation, this warming tea settles queasy stomachs (as fresh ginger is known to do) and warms and cheers tired campers.

2 TB grated fresh ginger *or* **2 TB chopped candied ginger or a combination of the two**
2 quarts boiling water

In Camp: Grate fresh ginger or chop candied ginger into a pot of boiling water. Cover for about 7 minutes and serve.

Dr. E's Russian Tea

This tasty, energizing drink mix is delicious hot or cold.

1 cup Tang
⅔ cup instant tea
½ cup sugar
¼ cup unsweetened lemonade mix
½ tsp ground cinnamon
¼ tsp ground cloves

At Home: Mix together ingredients and package amount needed for your trip.

In Camp: Use 2-3 teaspoons of mix per cup of water.

12

Breads and Baked Goods

There are all kinds of store-bought crackers that travel well in your backpack. Hard crackers such as Ry-Krisp, Wasa, and Sailor Boy Pilot Bread keep for a very long time.

Whole grain breads generally stay fresh longer than white loaves, such as French bread and they provide you with more energy for the trail, too. Pita bread, English muffins, and bagels are sturdy and versatile. But some breads can mold in their plastic bags after a few days so—although some may find this shocking—I often seek out breads for backpacking that contain the preservative calcium propionate, a mold inhibitor.

The recipes in this chapter are in two sections. The *Make Ahead Breads and Baked Goods* recipes are hearty, long-lasting breads and baked goodies to make at home. *Breads to Make on the Trail* recipes are basic, easy-to-make breads to bake in camp. You'll also find more baked goods in the *Desserts* chapter.

**Make
Ahead
Breads and
Baked
Goods**

You can customize your home-baked breads and cakes for traveling by baking them in your cooking pots or in a small tin that fits neatly in your pack. Because these sturdy high-energy breads, cakes, and trail snacks contain more sugar (a natural preservative) than most breads, they'll keep for well over a week and can be a welcome change from a steady diet of trail mix. Some of the recipes probably make more than you'll want to carry, but you can store extra loaves in the freezer for your next trip.

Mer's Prune Cake

Makes one 8" square cake

This sturdy cake is my grandmother's recipe. Frosted, it makes a good birthday cake on the trail, just plain it's an energizing trail snack. This cake tastes best several days after it's baked.

½ cup margarine
1 cup sugar
2 eggs
1 cup chopped prunes
1 tsp baking soda
½ cup prune juice
1 cup whole wheat flour
½ cup white flour
½ tsp salt
1 tsp baking powder
2 TB unsweetened cocoa powder
1 tsp vanilla
1 cup chopped walnuts

Pineapple Frosting
1 cup powdered sugar *or* 4 oz light cream cheese
½ cup crushed pineapple

At Home:
1. Cream margarine, sugar, and eggs. Stir in chopped prunes. 2. Dissolve baking soda in prune juice and add alternately to sifted dry ingredients and egg mixture, stirring all the while. Add vanilla and beat well. Stir in nuts and bake in an oiled 8"

square pan for 1 hour at 350 degrees. Or bake in smaller backpack-sized loaf pans for less time. (The time depends on the size of the pans. When a toothpick inserted in the center comes out clean the cake is done.) **3.** Remove from oven, and let cool for about an hour. Remove from pan, let cool completely, wrap in heavy-duty aluminum foil, and pack in a cooking pot for protection. If you've baked it in a small tin that you can carry in your pack, return it to the tin when cool.

In Camp: If you want to frost the prune cake, open a small can of crushed pineapple and add about ½ cup of powdered sugar. The frosting should be thin enough to drip down the sides of the cake, yet thick enough to coat the top. Let frosting set for about 15 minutes before serving. This is a very sweet frosting; you can also use light cream cheese—thin with crushed pineapple till spreadable. Please note that frosting amount depends on the size of your cake.

Lemon Loaf Cake

Makes one 8" square cake

This cake stays fresh for a long time and makes a perfect dessert after a spicy meal.

⅓ cup butter, melted
1 cup sugar
1 tsp lemon extract
¼ cup fresh lemon juice
2 eggs
1 cup whole wheat flour
Optional: 1½ tsp wheat gluten
½ cup white flour
1 tsp baking powder
1 tsp salt
½ cup milk
finely grated rind of 1 large lemon (don't grate
    deep enough to reach the pith, or white part)

Lemon Glaze
1 cup powdered sugar
¾ cup fresh lemon juice

At Home: 1. Preheat oven to 350 degrees. Cream together butter, sugar, lemon extract and juice. Beat in eggs well. Sift dry ingredients and stir in alternately with milk. Stir in lemon rind. 2. Pour into an oiled 8-inch loaf pan and bake for 1 hour. Or bake in backpack-sized loaf pans for less time. (The time depends on the size of the pots. When a toothpick inserted in the center comes out clean the cake is done.) 3. A few minutes before cake is done, make the glaze: Dissolve powdered sugar in lemon juice over low heat. When cake is done remove from oven and pierce about 20 holes all over the top with a toohpick or a meat fork. Then pour glaze over the top. Cool in pan for about an hour, then remove, let cool completely, wrap in heavy-duty aluminum foil, and pack in a cooking pot for protection. If you've baked it in a small tin that you can carry in your pack, return it to the tin when cool.

Jono's Herb Rolls
Makes 16 rolls

These are good for lunch with cheese or with a pesto dinner, and they still taste good several days down the trail.

2 TB finely chopped onions
⅓ cup sun-dried tomatoes, rehydrated and diced
1 TB finely chopped garlic
1 tsp dried oregano
2 TB butter
1 cup warm water (about 110 degrees)
2 tsp yeast
½ tsp salt
1 tsp sugar
1 cup white flour
1 cup whole wheat flour

At Home: 1. Sauté onions, sun-dried tomatoes, garlic, and oregano in butter till onions are translucent. Set aside. **2.** Dissolve yeast in warm water, stir in salt, sugar and sautéed tomatoes, herbs and onions. Add 1¾ cups flour, beat till smooth. Mix remaining flour to make dough easy to handle. **3.** Knead on lightly floured board till smooth and elastic, about 5 minutes. Place in greased bowl, turn greased side up, cover and let rise 30 minutes or until double. **4.** Punch down dough and divide into 16 balls. Brush with beaten egg white and place on greased cookie sheet. Let rise 30 minutes before baking, then bake for 30 minutes at 350 degrees.

Oat Date Bread

Makes two 8" loaves

2 cups chopped dates (Medjool dates if possible)
2 cups rolled oats
2 cups boiling water
2 eggs
¼ cup brown sugar
1½ cups whole wheat flour
2 tsp baking powder
1 tsp baking soda

1 cup oat flour
½ cup whole wheat flour
¼ cup grape *or* other sweet juice

1-1½ cups chopped walnuts

At Home: 1. Preheat oven to 350 degrees. Pour boiling water over dates and oats. **2.** Beat eggs till light; add sugar to eggs and continue to beat. **3.** Add first whole wheat flour, baking powder and baking soda to eggs and sugar and add half of the date-oat mixture. Stir in oat flour-whole wheat flour-juice mixture, then add rest of date-oat mixture and stir in walnuts. **4.** Put bread in oven and turn it down to 325 degrees. Bake for at least 1½ hours. Or bake in smaller backpack-sized loaf pans for less time. (The time depends on the size of the pots. When a toothpick inserted in the center comes out clean the cake is done.) When done this bread will be chewy on the outside, moist on the inside. Make sure this heavy bread is cooked all the way through. The first time I made it I cut the loaf in half 15 minutes after removing it from the oven and realized that it wasn't done—so I simply put it back in the oven and it was fine. **5.** Proceed with packing as for *Mer's Prune Cake*, step 3.

Buckwheat Molasses Mountain Bread

Makes two 8" loaves

Some nutritionists these days are telling us that buckwheat sticks to your ribs longer than other complex carbohydrates. Try this hearty bread instead of trail mix.

3 cups buttermilk
2½ tsp baking soda
1 cup whole wheat flour
2 cups buckwheat flour
Optional: 4 TB wheat gluten
1 cup rolled oats
⅓ cup oat bran
1 tsp salt
½ cup blackstrap molasses
1 cup currants
1 cup sunflower seeds

At Home: 1. Preheat oven to 350 degrees. Combine buttermilk and baking soda and blend in dry ingredients. Stir in molasses, then add currants and sunflower seeds. 2. Bake in two oiled 8" loaf pans for 1 hour at 350 degrees. Or bake in smaller backpack-sized loaf pans for less time. (The time depends on the size of the pots. When a toothpick inserted in the center comes out clean the cake is done.) 3. Proceed with packing as with *Mer's Prune Cake* from step 3.

Peggy's Date Sticks
Makes 12 sticks

We lose potassium when exercising, and dates contain potassium. This is my mother's recipe for a trail snack with a purpose.

3 eggs
1 cup sugar
1 cup whole wheat flour
½ tsp salt
1 tsp baking powder
1½ cup chopped dates
1 cup chopped nuts
Optional: powdered sugar

At Home: 1. In a mixing bowl, cream together eggs and sugar. **2.** Sift together flour, salt, and baking powder and fold into eggs and sugar. Stir in chopped dates and nuts. **3.** Bake in greased 9" x 13" pan for 35 minutes at 350 degrees. **4.** While the date bars are still warm, cut into 1" x 3½" pieces and generously dust with powdered sugar if desired.

Madeline's Jam Squares
Makes one 8" square pan

A fine dessert with a cup of tea.

¾ cup unsalted butter *or* margarine
¾ cup sugar
¼ tsp salt
1 tsp vanilla
1 egg
2 cups whole wheat flour
½ cup chopped walnuts
1½ cups flaked sweetened coconut
1 cup jam: apricot, raspberry, or blackberry

At Home: 1. Cream together butter, sugar, salt and vanilla. Add egg, flour, walnuts, and coconut. **2.** Spread half the mixture in a greased 8" square pan. Spread jam on top. Crumble the other half of the dough over the jam, it doesn't have to cover it completely. **3.** Bake at 350 degrees for about 40 minutes. Cool before cutting.

Breads to
Make
On the
Trail

Few things taste better to backpackers than fresh-baked bread in camp, and few things are more rewarding to the cook. These basic breads are pretty easy to make. See the section in *Chapter 7* "Baking on a Backpacking Stove" for more information on how to bake bread in camp.

Buttermilk Cornbread
Makes 8-10 servings

I prefer using the steaming method with this cornbread, even though it takes longer. You won't get a browned crust, but it comes out moist and with a cake-like texture.

1 cup yellow cornmeal
½ cup whole wheat flour
½ cup white flour
1 TB baking powder
¼ cup powdered egg
4 TB powdered buttermilk *or* ¼ cup dry milk
¼ cup sugar
⅓ cup safflower oil
1¼ cup water

At Home: Combine dry ingredients in a plastic bag. Add oil to main supply.

In Camp: **1.** Combine all ingredients and mix well. **2.** Pour into oiled 3-quart pot and steam for 30-45 minutes or pour into a Banks Frybake Pan and bake for 20-30 minutes. *Note:* You can cut this recipe in half for 2-4 servings, but don't double the recipe if you're using the steaming method—it would take a long, long time to cook.

Dixie's Baking Powder Biscuits

Makes eight 3" biscuits

Because biscuits should be baked at a high heat, the mini-oven method works best here. The steaming method will do, but biscuits will take a long time to bake. Before you start making these biscuits, find a surface to knead the dough. A flat, glacier-polished rock is perfect.

1 cup whole wheat flour
1 cup white flour
½ tsp salt
4 tsp baking powder
½ tsp cream of tartar
Optional: 2 TB sugar
¼ cup flour for kneading biscuits
scant ½ cup butter
¼ cup dry milk mixed with water to make ½ cup
¼ cup water

At Home: Combine dry ingredients. Add butter to main supply. Put dry milk and extra flour in separate ziploc bags.

In Camp: 1. Cut butter into dry ingredients. In camp you can use two knives or rub lumps between your fingers till dough is about the consistency of coarse cornmeal. 2. Stir milk into dough all at once. Add water—a bit more if dough is too dry. 3. Turn dough onto lightly floured surface and knead gently and quickly. Fold the dough only about 8 times. Roll out dough using a liter-size nalgene bottle as a rolling pin. You can use the mouth of the bottle as a biscuit cutter, too. 4. Put cut biscuits into a lightly-oiled Banks Frybake Pan (or equivalent), setting as far apart as room allows so they'll bake faster. Bake for 20-30 minutes with stove set on simmer and twig fire on top.

Camper's Coffee Cake

Makes 8-10 servings

This recipe seems to be foolproof, and it's ready to bake in about 10 minutes.

1 cup whole wheat flour
¾ cup white flour
Optional: 2 tsp wheat gluten
scant ¼ cup dry milk
¼ cup powdered egg
½ cup brown sugar
¼ tsp salt
4 tsp baking powder
⅓ cup oil
1 cup water

Topping
⅓ cup brown sugar
1 tsp cinnamon
2 TB flour
½ cup walnuts
4 TB melted butter

At Home: Measure and mix together dry ingredients for cake and place in a plastic bag. Add oil and butter to main supply. In a separate bag mix first 3 filling ingredients together; package nuts in a separate bag.

In Camp: **1.** Melt butter and stir in filling ingredients. Set aside. **2.** Add oil and water to cake's dry ingredients and mix together till just blended. Pour half of this mixture into oiled pan for steaming. Spread filling mixture on top and add the rest of the cake batter. Sprinkle nuts on top. **3.** Bake for about 20-30 minutes with the mini-oven method. Increase cooking time if you use the steaming method.

Variation: Substitute almonds or macadamia nuts for walnuts; top with jam (raspberry is good), marmalade, stewed fruit, or *Strawberry Sauce* (page 215).

Rogue River Bread

Makes 1 Dutch loaf

In the spring of 1974 I decided to get out of the city for awhile. I quit law school and ended up working for the Forest Service on the Rogue River in Oregon. Down the road from my cabin a Viet Nam vet was making a peaceful new life for himself as a caretaker for a beautiful little spread owned by the BLM. He had a Jersey cow and once a week he'd bring me milk and I'd bake bread. While the bread baked he'd shake a jar of cream till it turned to butter. When the bread came out of the oven we'd slather it with sweet butter and eat and talk. Then he'd take home his loaf of bread and I'd have fresh milk and butter. Here is that bread recipe simplified for the trail.

> 2 cups whole wheat flour
> 1¼ cups white flour
> 1 TB wheat gluten
> ¼ cup white flour (for dusting kneading surface)
> ¼ cup egg powder
> 2 TB vegetable oil
> 1 tsp salt
> ¼ cup sugar
> 1 pkg dry yeast (Rapid-rise type if possible)
> 1¼ cups water (105 to 115 degrees)

At Home: In a ziploc bag package the flours, wheat gluten, and egg powder. Package the sugar and salt in a separate ziploc bag (do not package salt and sugar with other dry ingredients, they'll help activate the yeast when you combine them in camp). In yet another plastic bag, package ¼ cup flour. Include 2 TB oil and some extra oil with main supply for oiling baking pan. Package together in a larger ziploc and include the package of yeast.

In Camp: You'll have best results if you make this bread on a sunny, lazy day in camp. Yeast breads need to be babied a bit and should be kept free of drafts and sudden temperature changes. **1.** In a 3-quart pot dissolve yeast in warm water—it should feel warm to the fingertips. Add sugar and salt, stir once and let it stand for 1-2 minutes. **2.** Stir in oil, add a bit less than half the flour mixture and beat with a wooden spoon till smooth. Mix in remaining flour till dough is easy to handle. **3.** Turn dough onto a lightly floured surface and knead until smooth and elastic, about 8-10 minutes. A warm flat rock would be perfect for this; if the rock is cold, a towel and a large plastic bag make a good kneading surface. **4.** In the meantime, wash out the pot and coat with oil. Form the dough in a smooth Dutch loaf shape and place in pot, oiled side up. Cover with a cloth and set in a warm place (about 80 degrees) to rise for about an hour. Dough is ready when double in bulk or an impression made with your thumb remains. **5.** Punch down dough and shape into a loaf the size of your baking pan. You can use the Banks Frybake Pan or a 3-quart pot. (Adjust cooking time to the size of your pot.) Cover and let rise again for about 45 minutes. **6.** Bake for 30-40 minutes using the mini-oven method. The steaming method produces a lovely bread but it must be cooked a long time—an hour is not too long. If you attempt this method above 8000' bread may stay raw in the middle.

Variation: Add ¾ cup raisins in Step 2 when you add the remaining flour.

13

Salads and Side Dishes

After a few days on the trail, most people start hankering for a a crisp salad. Even a green leaf salad is possible out in the wilderness, and a piquant vinaigrette dressing will enliven your entire meal.

Carrots, jicama, onions, snow peas, apples, oranges, and avocados are good trail salad makings, too. Most fresh salad ingredients are heavy, but just a small amount is greatly satisfying to a backpacker with a craving for fresh vegetables.

If you want to go for light weight, dried carrots and cabbage rehydrate to make surprisingly fresh-tasting crunchy salads. Pasta, grain, and bean salads are a great way to use leftovers and give backpackers those much-needed carbos, too.

Oja Salad

The ingredients of this simple but elegant salad keep for several days without refrigeration. They're a bit heavy— but a much-appreciated treat after several days away from civilization. Even if you can't find watercress in camp, the salad is still delicious.

2 oranges
1 apple (preferably Granny Smith)
1 small jicama (enough to yield ½ cup jicama cut
    in matchsticks)
1 cup loosely-packed watercress (if available in
    camp)
Oriental Dressing (see below)

At Home: Package oranges, apple and a small jicama in brown paper bags. Make *Oriental Dressing* and put in small nalgene bottle. Toast sesame seeds.

In Camp: 1. Peel oranges, slice into ¼" horizontal rounds, then into small wedge-shaped pieces. Core apple, peel if you wish and cut in same way as orange. 2. Peel jicama and cut into thin matchsticks. If there is an abundance of watercress growing near your camp, by all means add it to the salad. 3. Toss with *Oriental Dressing* and sprinkle toasted sesame seeds on top.

Oriental Dressing
¼ tsp sugar
¼ cup fresh lime juice
1 scant TB finely chopped candied ginger
1 tsp sesame oil
¼ cup safflower oil
salt and pepper
toasted sesame seeds (about 1 TB, more if desired)

At Home: Combine all ingredients but sesame seeds in a nalgene bottle. If you are planning to use this dressing after several days on the trail, don't add the lime juice until ready to eat. Limes keep almost indefinitely; the skins form a hard shell, but they stay fresh and juicy inside for some time. If you don't want to carry a lime, orange-flavored Tang will do as a substitute. Package toasted sesame seeds in a small nalgene bottle or plastic film can.

How to toast sesame seeds: Sesame seeds are usually raw when you buy them and the flavor is greatly improved by toasting in a toaster oven or heating in a nonstick skillet over medium-low heat until toasty brown. They burn easily, so watch them carefully.

How to clean watercress: If you're gathering watercress from water sources that may be contaminated by giardia or other "bugs," rinse and clean by soaking it in iodine-treated water (10 drops of iodine per liter of water) in a bucket or cooking pot for 20-30 minutes. To rid watercress of the taste of iodine, rinse well in plain filtered water.

Green Salads

The greens you use in a green salad on the trail depend on how many days you've been out. For the first or possibly second night, you can enjoy a mix of baby lettuce greens. Arugula is a gourmet lettuce I've been able to keep without refrigeration until the third night of a backpacking trip.

Hard-core gourmets turn their noses up at iceberg lettuce, but it's great for backpacking and will stay crisp four or five days. Cabbage has the longest life of all, up to a week or more.

The secret lies in the packing: Don't wash, don't cut, and *don't pack in plastic.* Use brown paper bags. You'll probably have to discard some of the outer leaves, but you may be surprised at how long lettuce and other vegetables stay fresh using this simple packing method. For more information, see *Chapter 5, Packing Food and Keeping It Fresh.*

A plastic bag makes a good salad bowl in camp. An outstanding salad dressing is Marukan seasoned gourmet rice vinegar with no oil, just plain. (If you can't find Marukan, look for a rice vinegar diluted to 4.1 acidity with a little added salt and sugar.)

Blood Oranges and Capers With Spring-Mix Baby Lettuces
Makes 6 servings

This salad is quite extravagant for a backpacking trip. Impressive, too.

> 2 blood oranges *or* 2 navel or other oranges
> ¼ cup capers
> 4 cups Spring Mix: a mixture of arugula, rocket,
>   endive, red, romaine and other baby lettuces
> *Dijon-Balsamic Vinaigrette* (see below)

At Home: 1. Package capers in a small nalgene bottle. 2. Prepare the *Dijon-Balsamic Vinaigrette* and package in a nalgene bottle. Since you're eating this salad the first night you can package lettuce in plastic bags. 3. Put lettuce and oranges inside cooking pots to save them from getting crushed.

In Camp: 1. Put *Spring Mix* on a platter. A big piece of heavy-duty aluminum foil shaped like a platter does nicely. 2. Peel and slice blood oranges in rounds and arrange them on the bed of lettuce. 3. Sprinkle capers over oranges and then sprinkle dressing over all.

Dijon-Balsamic Vinaigrette
Makes 1 cup

This is a wonderful dressing over lettuce or cabbage and it perks up leftover beans, rice, or pasta.

> 1 tsp Dijon mustard
> 1 garlic clove, crushed
> 2 TB balsamic vinegar
> ¼ cup Marukan seasoned gourmet rice vinegar
> ¾ cup olive oil
> ⅛ tsp freshly ground pepper
> salt

At Home: Combine ingredients in a nalgene bottle and shake to mix. The garlic clove should be removed after 24 hours.

Sunflower-Caraway Cabbage Salad

Makes 4 servings

Cabbage keeps beautifully without refrigeration. However, it is heavy so if you don't want to carry the extra weight try dehydrated cabbage. It's not as crisp as fresh cabbage, but does a pretty good job of satisfying a craving for a crunchy salad.

2 oz dehydrated shredded cabbage, red or green *or*
1 small head cabbage
¼ cup sunflower seeds, toasted and salted
2 tsp caraway seeds
Optional: ¼ cup dehydrated apples

Cabbage Salad Dressing
¼ cup safflower oil
¼ cup balsamic vinegar
1 tsp brown sugar
2 TB soy sauce

At Home: 1. If dehydrated cabbage is used, package with apples (if used) in plastic bag. 2. Sunflower and caraway seeds can be packaged together. 3. Combine dressing ingredients in a nalgene bottle.

In Camp: 1. Rehydrate cabbage and apples in warm water. 2. Drain well, add seeds, and toss with dressing. *Note:* The cabbage should be raw when dehydrated, not cooked.

Havasu Watercress Salmon

Makes 4 servings

I serve this salad on our trip to the Havasu Indian Reservation in the Grand Canyon, where Havasu Creek is loaded with wild watercress. If you can't gather watercress, iceberg lettuce will do as a substitute.

8 oz-can salmon
1 small red onion, cut in rings
2 TB capers
1 fresh lemon, cut in wedges
Garnish: 5-6 sprigs fresh dill *or* **½ tsp dried dill**
watercress

At Home: 1. In separate brown paper bags package onion, fresh dill (if used), and lemon. **2.** Put capers in a small nalgene bottle. **3.** Pack canned salmon.

In Camp: 1. Gather watercress and rinse according to directions on page 139. **2.** Cut onion rings and lemon in wedges. Make a bed of watercress and arrange onion rings and salmon on watercress. **3.** Sprinkle with capers, squeeze a couple of wedges of lemon on salmon, garnish with dill (or sprinkle dried dill over top) and remaining lemon wedges.

Chinese Grain Salad

Makes 4 servings

1 cup rice (quick brown rice, Basmati, Minute Rice
    or **any grain or pasta)**
1 TB oriental sesame oil
¼ cup Marukan seasoned gourmet rice vinegar
2 TB soy sauce
2 tsp grated ginger
24 snow peas
½ oz dried, shredded carrots
½ oz dried sweet peppers, red or green, diced
Optional: 1 cup vacuum-packed tofu, firm variety

At Home: 1. Package rice in sealable plastic bag. Combine soy, sesame oil, and rice vinegar in a small nalgene bottle. **2.** Add ginger root to spice bag. Package snow peas in brown paper bag. Dehydrated veggies may be packaged together. Pack tofu (if used).

In Camp: 1. Cook rice according to directions. Trim snow peas and add them to dehydrated vegetables, then rehydrate vegetables with hot water; this will also cook the snowpeas just slightly. **2.** While rice is still slightly warm, mix in liquids, grate in fresh ginger, and stir in snow peas and rehydrated vegetables. **3.** Gently stir in diced tofu and serve.

Mexican Tabouli

Makes 6 servings

1 cup bulgur wheat
2 cups boiling water
Spice Packet:
   1 tsp cumin
   1 tsp pasilla *or* other mild chili powder
   ½ tsp oregano
¼ cup olive oil
½ cup Marukan seasoned gourmet rice vinegar
¼ cup freeze-dried corn
1 TB dehydrated carrots, grated or sliced
1 tsp dehydrated celery
1 red, green, or yellow sweet peppers, cut in thin
   strips and dehydrated *or* 2 tsp bell pepper flakes
¼ cup dehydrated beans *or* 1 5-oz can beans (kidney or garbanzo)
Optional: 1 jalapeño pepper, seeded, deveined and
   minced
1 small jicama, enough to equal 1 cup, diced
1 tsp Tabasco sauce or to taste
3 fresh green onions, minced
⅓ cup *South of the Border Pesto* (page 179)
   and eliminate the olive oil) *or* 1 cup chopped
   fresh cilantro

At Home: 1. Package all dehydrated vegetables together in a boilable plastic bag. Package all produce in brown paper bags. 2. Combine olive oil and rice vinegar in a nalgene bottle. Combine spices in a packet. 3. Put bulgur in a ziploc or boilable bag. Bring small nalgene container of Tabasco sauce.

In Camp: 1. Boil 2 cups water and pour over bulgur. Cover and soak for about an hour. When bulgur is tender, drain and press out excess water. Meanwhile, rehydrate vegetables. 2. Stir spices, then vegetables into bulgur. 3. Add olive oil (if used) and rice vinegar, jalapeño pepper, green onions and *South of the Border Pesto* or cilantro. 4. Add Tabasco sauce to taste. Let it marinate for a while if you can.

Carrot-Raisin Salad
Makes 4 servings

You may be surprised at the fresh, crisp taste of this salad made from dehydrated carrots.

4 oz dehydrated shredded carrots (about 4 large
    carrots)
¾ cup raisins
2½ oz dried pineapple (about 4 slices), diced

At Home: Package carrots in a sealable plastic bag and raisins and pineapple in another plastic bag.

In Camp: 1. Rehydrate carrots, pineapple, and raisins together in warm but not boiling water. 2. When salad has cooled and carrots are rehydrated, drain and eat. Reserve rehydrating water for a delicious carrot juice drink.

Spicy Cumin Carrots
Makes 4 servings

This can be served as hot side dish or eaten cold as a crunchy salad. It would be excellent served with a meat curry or with the Indian Sambaar Stew *on page 192 .*

4 oz dehydrated thinly sliced carrots (about 4 large
    fresh carrots)
½ chicken bouillon cube
2 fresh green onions *or* 2 tsp dehydrated onions
⅛ -¼ tsp Tabasco sauce
1-2 cloves finely minced fresh garlic
1 tsp cumin seeds *or* ½ tsp powdered cumin
salt and pepper
Optional: ½ cup fresh minced cilantro

At Home: 1. Measure dehydrated vegetables into plastic bags and package fresh vegetables in brown paper bags; add garlic and Tabasco sauce to main supply 2. package packet of cumin with chicken bouillon cube.

In Camp: 1. Rehydrate carrots with hot water to cover into which half a chicken bouillon cube has been dissolved. Set aside. 2. When carrots have rehydrated, drain chicken broth and add cumin, minced garlic, green onions, and tabasco sauce. **3.** Eat as a hot side dish or allow to cool. Just before serving stir in cilantro and salt and pepper to taste.

Onion Rings Vinaigrette

Makes 4 servings

In Hawaii I make this salad with mild, sweet Maui onions. On the mainland look for Walla Walla, Texas sweet, or other mild onions.

2 medium-size mild onions

Dressing:
½ **tsp dillweed**
¼ **cup apple cider vinegar**
½ **cup safflower oil**
salt and pepper

At Home: Package the onions in brown paper bags. Combine the dill, cider vinegar, oil, salt and pepper and put in a small nalgene bottle.

In Camp: **1.** Peel onions and slice horizontally in ⅛-¼" thick rings. **2.** Pour dressing over onions and if possible allow to marinate for 2 to 4 hours.

Captain Chris's Avocado

Makes 2 servings

Avocado with Worcestershire sauce may not sound appetizing, but it's really quite delicious—and so simple.

1 avocado
4 TB olive oil
2 TB Worcestershire sauce

At Home: Combine olive oil and Worcestershire sauce and put in a nalgene bottle. Package avocado in brown paper bag.

In Camp: **1.** When avocado is ripe, cut in half lengthwise and remove seed. **2.** Pour olive oil-Worcestershire sauce mixture in seed wells and eat with a spoon.

Dilled Baby Lima Salad
Makes 4 servings

This bean salad is great for a lunch in camp on a rest day, or as a side dish accompanying grilled meat. For the dressing, use a fragrant, cold-pressed peanut oil.

2 cups cooked dehydrated lima beans

Dressing:
¼ **cup safflower oil**
¼ **cup peanut oil**
1 TB fresh dill *or* ½ **tsp dried dillweed**
⅓ **cup Marukan seasoned gourmet rice vinegar**

At Home: Package the dehydrated beans in ziploc bag. Combine the dressing ingredients and put in a nalgene bottle.

In Camp: **1.** Rehydrate beans with just barely enough water to cover. Be careful not to add too much water. **2.** When beans are rehydrated, drain off excess water and add dressing. If possible, marinate for 2-4 hours before eating.

14

Soups

Soup is always good, and it really hits the spot when you're camping. Many backpackers plan soup with every meal because it's fast and it holds hunger pangs at bay while the rest of dinner cooks.

There are some good soup mixes on the market and some pretty terrible ones, too. Adding fresh vegetables and spices to some commercial soup mixes not only disguises the processed taste, but makes a tasty pot of soup. For example, you can use Kikkoman's Hot and Sour Soup mix as a base and add soy sauce, rice vinegar and all kinds of fresh vegetables with delicious results. Use Knorr's Tomato Soup mix with basil as a base for minestrone or simply add a shot of dry sherry to Knorr's Oxtail Soup mix for a gourmet touch.

To dress up packaged miso soup mixes, add a touch of sesame oil and grated fresh ginger; stir a fresh egg and green onions into Kikkoman's Egg Flower Soup mix; or add fresh vegetables and pesto to Top Ramen. The simple addition of grated onion or a dash of Tabasco sauce can enliven a pre-packaged soup, and don't underestimate the humble bouillon cube. Beef, fish, vegetable, or chicken bouillon cubes make a good soup base, and drunk just plain the salty broth quickly restores feelings of well-being after a strenuous day on the trail.

Here are recipes for soups to make on the trail— some are classic old favorites and some are exotic. Many of the recipes call for bouillon cubes. I prefer Knorr brand, which makes 2 cups bouillon for 1 cube. You can, of course, substitute fresh vegetables for dehydrated or freeze-dried in any of the recipes.

Marrakech Soup

Makes 4 servings

This refreshing, lemony African soup enlivened with warming spices will take the edge off big appetites after a long day on the trail.

2 chicken bouillon cubes
1 TB minced, dried celery *or* ⅛ tsp celery seeds
1 large clove garlic, sliced
1 TB dried leeks *or* onions
4 lemon slices (dried or fresh)
¼ tsp ground ginger
¼ tsp ground turmeric
¼ tsp ground cinnamon
Optional: pinch crushed saffron
4 cups water

At Home: Put all dry ingredients in ziploc bag.

In Camp: 1. Peel and slice garlic clove and add all ingredients to water. 2. Bring to boil, then turn down heat and cover. Simmer for 15 minutes; the longer it simmers the better it gets.

Menu Suggestions: For a main-dish soup add rice and serve with whole wheat bread. *Lemon Loaf Cake* is excellent for dessert.

Dahl Shorba

Makes 8 servings

People love this curried lentil soup. It takes more preparation time than most trail dinners, so I usually make it on a rest day and serve it with chutney and fresh-baked Buttermilk Cornbread.

8 cups water
4 chicken broth cubes
2 cups lentils (*Masoor Dahl*, see Note below)
1 fresh onion *or* 1/3 cup dried onion
2 cloves garlic, minced
2 TB curry powder
2 TB fresh grated ginger
2 tsp coriander seeds
1/4 tsp red pepper flakes
olive oil
4 TB butter
1/4 cup dry milk plus 1/2 cup water
Garnish: lemon slices

At Home: Package lentils in a ziploc bag. Put onion and garlic in a paper bag and label. Combine spices and package together. Include olive oil, butter and dry milk with main supply.

In Camp: 1. Combine water, chicken broth cubes, and lentils. Bring to boil, reduce heat and cover. Cook on medium-low heat for 20 minutes; remove from heat and set aside. The lentils will continue to cook even though they're not on the heat. They should be cooked through before starting step two. 2. Dice onion, mince garlic, grate ginger, and cook and stir in oil together with curry, crushed coriander seeds and red pepper flakes. Cook over medium heat for 7 minutes. Stir spice mixture into lentils. Cover. Cook over medium-low heat for another 20 minutes. 3. Just before serving stir in butter and milk and heat through. Garnish with lemon slices. *Note:* For this recipe you need the quick-cooking little salmon-colored lentils found in Indian grocery stores called *Masoor Dahl*. These lentils when cooked turn pale yellow, and they cook in about half the time of other lentils.

Savory Lentil Soup
Makes 4 servings

I don't know why lentils make such good soup. Maybe it's because they're both comforting and hearty.

2 cups cooked and dehydrated brown lentils
5-6 cups water
2 beef bouillon cubes
2 TB sliced or shredded dehydrated carrots
1 TB dehydrated celery *or* ¼ tsp crushed celery
  seeds
2 TB dehydrated leeks *or* onions
1 clove garlic, minced
1 bay leaf
2 whole cloves
2 TB Worcestershire sauce
dash cayenne
salt and pepper
Optional: ½ cup diced smoked tofu or ham; or
  sliced Polish or other sausage

At Home: Put dehydrated lentils in a ziploc bag. Combine in another ziploc the carrots, celery, leeks, unpeeled garlic, bay leaf, and cloves. Put Worcestershire sauce in a small nalgene bottle. Package optional tofu, ham or sausage in brown paper bag.

In Camp: **1.** Rehydrate vegetables in 4 cups water, add garlic and bouillon cubes. Cook at medium-low for a few minutes. **2.** Add dehydrated lentils and if necessary add more water to soup. Add optional meat or tofu, dash cayenne, and adjust seasonings. **3.** Cook till flavors mingle, about 15 minutes.

Baby Lima-Dill Soup

Makes 4 servings

*This quick and easy soup calls for dehydrated lima beans.
The dill imparts a rich buttery flavor to the baby limas.
Smoked Gouda cheese and a hearty whole-wheat bread
are a delicious complement.*

2 cups cooked and dehydrated baby lima beans
4-5 cups water
2 TB dried leeks *or* **1 small fresh onion**
2 tsp dillweed
salt and pepper
1 TB butter
3 TB Marukan seasoned gourmet rice vinegar

At Home: Package leeks and dillweed together. Put in a larger
ziploc with packaged dehydrated baby limas. Add
butter and rice vinegar to main supply.

In Camp: **1.** Rehydrate baby limas in 4 cups water; crush
about half of them in your hands before adding the
rehydrating water. Some beans should be powdered to thicken the soup and some beans should
retain their shape. **2.** Simmer beans and add leeks,
dillweed, pepper and salt. If necessary, add more
water, but this should be a thick soup. Stir in butter.
A few minutes before serving stir in Marukan seasoned gourmet rice vinegar.

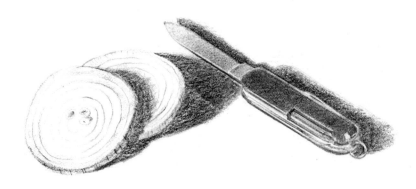

Thai Tom Yum

Makes 8 servings

This is the wonderful lemongrass-coconut-milk soup served in Thai restaurants, and it's my very favorite soup. We've eaten it on snowy winter evenings in our ski hut in the Tahoe Sierra and on hot-weather backpacking trips in the Grand Canyon. It may seem like a complicated dish because of the unfamiliar ingredients, but these foods are easily found in any Thai grocery store.

2 chicken bouillon cubes
2 50-gram packages Yeo's unsweetened coconut
    cream powder *or* 2 cups canned coconut milk
1 4-5 inch clump lemongrass, chopped in ¼" pieces
3 lime leaves
Optional: 3 or 4 cilantro roots, crushed
3-4 slices galanga (looks like fresh ginger)
2 TB Thai chili paste
4 TB fish sauce
8-10 cups water
Vegetables:
    ½ cup dried mushrooms
    16 canned baby corn spears
    10-15 strips dehydrated red or yellow bell peppers
    15 snow peas
    ½ cup freeze-dried peas
Garnish: 2 green onions, minced and ½ cup
    chopped cilantro leaves

At Home: Package bouillon cubes, lemongrass, lime leaves and galanga in a brown paper bag. Put cilantro roots and fresh vegetables in separate paper bags; package dehydrated vegetables together. Put chili paste and fish sauce in their own nalgene bottles.

In Camp: **1.** To 6 cups water add bouillon cubes, galanga, chili paste, fish sauce, crushed lime leaves, cilantro roots, chopped lemongrass, and dehydrated vegetables. Bring to a boil and lower to simmer for about 15 minutes. **2.** Mix coconut cream powder with 2 cups water and shake in a nalgene bottle to blend well. Add to soup. About 10 minutes before serving add fresh vegetables. Just before serving stir in chopped green onions and fresh cilantro.

Black Bean Soup

Makes 4 servings

4 cups water
7 oz package Fantastic Foods dried black beans; *or*
   7 oz home-dried black beans
¼ tsp thyme
1 bay leaf
1 clove garlic, minced
2 TB dried leeks *or* onions
2 TB olive oil
Optional: 2 TB dry sherry
   dollop of sour cream or plain yogurt for each serving

At Home: Package thyme, bay leaf, garlic, and leeks or onions together. Put optional sherry in nalgene bottle and put all in large ziploc with packaged black beans. Add oil to main supply. If you're bringing yogurt or sour cream, put the plastic container it comes in in a self-sealing bag without opening and keep chilled till you get to the trailhead. Obviously, this garnish can't be used if you planning this soup later than the first night of your trip and can't keep it chilled.

In Camp: 1. Mince garlic and combine with everything but optional sherry and sour cream or yogurt. 2. Cook soup for 15 minutes or so over medium heat. 3. Stir in sherry if desired, and—if you have it—add a dollop of yogurt or sour cream to each bowl of soup and serve.

Simple Oyster Stew with Paprika Butter

Makes 4 servings

This comforting and simple-to-make oyster stew is the meal to have when you're holed up in your cozy tent listening to the rain on the roof.

2 8-oz cans whole oysters
1 cup dry milk mixed with 3 cups water
salt and pepper
dash of Tabasco sauce
2 TB *Paprika Butter* (see below)
Garnish: chopped chives *or* green onions, fresh or dried

At Home: Package chive or green onion garnish; add Tabasco sauce to main supply; put *Paprika Butter* in large-mouth nalgene jar. Put all ingredients together in a large ziploc.

In Camp: 1. Combine the oyster liquid and milk in a 3-quart pot and bring to a simmer. 2. Add the oysters and cook gently only until edges curl or they are warmed through. Do not overcook oysters. 3. Season with salt and pepper, add a dash of Tabasco sauce and a sprinkle of chives or green onions—and just before serving stir in a couple of tablespoons of *Paprika Butter*.

Paprika Butter

¼ lb sweet butter
1 TB paprika
pinch cayenne pepper
pinch salt

Blend butter and spices, carry in a nalgene jar. Add to soups, spread on breads and crackers.

Leek and Potato Soup

Makes 6 servings

This quick and filling soup calls for instant potato flakes; try to use a health-food-store brand that isn't heavily loaded with salt. You can use dried onions instead of leeks, but leeks taste better.

3 cups water
2 chicken bouillon cubes
3-4 TB thinly sliced dried leeks; *or* one thinly
    sliced small leek; *or* ½ medium onion
1½ cups instant potato flakes
2-4 TB butter
1 cup dry milk mixed with 4 cups cold water
salt and pepper
Optional: 2 tsp dried parsley

At Home: Package leeks and instant potatoes in separate ziploc bags. Add butter and dry milk to main supply. Put potato and leek packages in a large ziploc with chicken bouillon cubes and dried parsley packet.

In Camp: 1. Bring 3 cups water to boil with bouillon cubes and leeks. Add butter and cold milk. Stir in potato flakes with fork or whisk. 2. Cook gently about 10 minutes or until leeks are tender; add more water if necessary. Salt and pepper to taste, and add parsley flakes if desired.

Quick Clam Chowder

Makes 6 servings

The instant potato flakes give this New England-style clam chowder a creamy, rich texture. A dash of Tabasco sauce makes this soup come alive, and it tastes great accompanied by humble little oyster crackers.

3 cups water
2 TB thinly sliced dried leeks *or* ½ thinly sliced
    small leek *or* ½ medium onion
2-4 TB butter
1 cup dry milk mixed with 4 cups cold water
1 cup instant potato flakes
6½-oz can minced clams with broth
Optional: 2 tsp dried parsley; ½ cup diced bacon
    or ham; 1 medium cooked potato, diced
dash Tabasco sauce
salt and pepper

At Home: Package leeks and instant potatoes in separate ziploc bags. Add butter, Tabasco sauce, and dry milk to main supply. Put potato and leek packages in large ziploc with canned clams and dried parsley packet.

In Camp: 1. Add 3 cups water to leeks and bring to boil. Add butter and cold milk. Stir in potato flakes with fork or whisk. Add clams and broth and optional diced potato, bacon or ham. 2. Cook gently about 10-15 minutes or until leeks are tender; add more water if necessary. Add a shot of Tabasco sauce; salt and pepper to taste. Stir in parsley flakes if desired.

French Onion Soup Gratinée

Makes 6 servings

This wonderfully extravagant soup turns dinner on the trail into a Bastille Day celebration. You could follow it with a simple stir-fry of zucchini, mushrooms, and garlic; or—for big appetites—ground round burgers and a green salad.

1 recipe *French Onion Soup Base*, dehydrated (page 168)
2 beef bouillon cubes
6-8 cups water
3 TB cognac *or* brandy
2 oz Swiss cheese
4-6 oz grated Parmesan cheese
salt and pepper
Optional: *Camper's Croutes* (see below)

At Home: Pack in a large ziploc bag the package of dehydrated soup base, beef bouillon cubes, small nalgene bottle of cognac or brandy, and separately packaged cheeses.

In Camp: **1.** Combine soup base, beef bouillon cubes and water and simmer gently for at least 10 minutes. Add salt and pepper to taste. **2.** Grate or thinly sliver Swiss cheese. Stir into soup. Immediately before serving stir in cognac or brandy and sprinkle with Parmesan cheese.

Variation: After stirring in Swiss cheese, float *Camper's Croutes* on top of soup and sprinkle Parmesan cheese all over surface of the soup. Put lid on pot and gently simmer for a few minutes until Parmesan has melted and formed a crust, then lift a corner with a spoon and stir in cognac or brandy. Serve immediately.

Camper's Croutes

You can make croutes ahead of time at home, or in camp.

Croutes make this French onion soup really special. They're also good with minestrone and in salads, and if you manage to have any left over they're great for lunch, too. Make a big batch if you like. They'll keep for at least a week.

> Bread slices, ½-¾" thick (French bread—white or whole wheat, fresh or slightly stale—is usually used but any bread will do)
> olive oil
> cut clove of garlic
> Parmesan cheese

At Home: 1. Bake bread slices on a cookie sheet in a 325 degree oven till very crisp and lightly browned, about 30 minutes. 2. Baste each side with a few drops of good olive oil as they're cooking. 3. After toasting, each piece may be rubbed with a cut clove of garlic and sprinkled with a little Parmesan cheese. 4. Wrap in aluminum foil.

In Camp: Toast bread in frying pan, turning over several times until crisp and crusty. Then continue with step 3 above.

Minestrone with Pesto

Makes 6 servings

Most people think of eating pesto only with pasta, but pesto adds a touch of genius to minestrone. You can use all dehydrated (or freeze-dried) vegetables in this recipe—or try a combination of fresh and dehydrated.

6-8 cups water
Optional: ½ cup dehydrated navy, kidney or cranberry beans
½ cup pasta: small bows *or* shells *or* Rosamarie (it looks like rice)
2 beef *or* chicken *or* vegetable bouillon cubes
3 oz dehydrated spaghetti sauce; *or* 1 tube double-concentrated Italian tomato paste; *or* 4 TB tomato powder
10 sun-dried tomatoes, diced
1 TB dehydrated leeks *or* 1 small fresh onion
1 TB diced dehydrated celery *or* 1 stalk fresh
2 TB sliced dehydrated carrot *or* 1 fresh carrot
3 TB dried mushrooms
½ cup dehydrated zucchini *or* 1 fresh zucchini
2 red and yellow bell peppers, fresh or dehydrated, cut in strips
2 garlic cloves, minced
1 tsp oregano leaves
2 TB parsley flakes
salt and pepper
Basil Pesto (page 178), 1-2 TB per person
Parmesan cheese, about 1 TB per person (grated)

At Home: Package dehydrated vegetables in one bag. Package all spices together. Beans and pasta can go together in one bag. Put Parmesan cheese in a ziploc. Pesto goes in a nalgene bottle. Put fresh veggies in separate brown paper bags.

In Camp: 1. Combine all dehydrated vegetables with hot water, bouillon cubes, spices, minced garlic and tomato paste and cook gently until vegetables are tender. 2. Combine fresh vegetables, optional beans, and pasta and simmer for about 15 minutes or until pasta is cooked. 3. Serve with a dollop of pesto and a sprinkling of grated Parmesan cheese in each cup of soup.

Swordfish Chowder

Makes 6 servings

Because all ingredients are fresh, this soup must be served the first night of your camping trip if you're not able to keep it chilled. It's a fast meal because most of the preparation is done at home.

1 TB butter
3 carrots, sliced
2 potatoes, cubed
2 onions, sliced
2 cloves
⅛ tsp fennel seeds, crushed
1 bay leaf
2 TB flour
½ cup water
1 lb swordfish, halibut, tuna, or shark fillets
1 TB fresh dill *or* **1 tsp dried dillweed**
½ cup dry white wine
½ cup dry milk mixed with 2 cups water
salt and pepper
Garnish: fresh parsley

At Home: 1. Sauté vegetables, cloves, crushed fennel seeds, and bay leaf in butter for 5 minutes. Stir in flour till blended, add ½ cup water, cover, simmer for 5 minutes and remove from heat. Vegetables should be slightly under-cooked. 2. When the vegetable mixture has cooled, package in a self-sealing bag and keep chilled till you get to the trailhead. 3. Package the rest of the ingredients: wine in a nalgene bottle, dry milk with main supply. Chop fresh dill and parsley, put in separate plastic bags and refrigerate. It's not necessary to freeze the fish since you're eating it the first night, but keep it chilled until you get to the trailhead.

In Camp: 1. Put vegetable mixture in 3-quart pot and simmer with dill and 2 cups water for 10 minutes or till vegetables are cooked. 2. Add fish, wine, and milk and simmer till fish is cooked, about 5 minutes. 3. Add salt and pepper if desired and sprinkle with fresh parsley.

First Night Soup

Makes 4 servings

This is the perfect soup for the first night out at high elevation, when people usually aren't very hungry. The crisp fresh vegetables are colorful and appealing to altitude-subdued appetites, and since they're all cut and ready to drop into the soup, dinner is easy and ready in just a few minutes.

1 package of Kikkoman Hot and Sour Soup mix
   (one that calls for 4 cups of water)
1 TB soy sauce
1 TB sesame oil
2 TB Marukan seasoned gourmet rice vinegar
4 cups water
vegetables in proportions of your choice to equal
about 4 cups:
   thinly sliced carrots
   snow peas
   celery
   bok choy
   peas
   bean sprouts
   shiitaki mushrooms
   green onions
   canned baby corn
   canned bamboo shoots
   Optional: cubed tofu

At Home: Cut, slice, and dice veggies and bag together in small ziplocs according to cooking times; for example, put slower cooking celery and carrots together, quick-cooking bean sprouts and snow peas together. Open cans and put corn and bamboo shoots in ziplocs and refrigerate. Soy sauce, rice vinegar, and sesame oil can be combined in one nalgene bottle or a self-sealing bag packet.

In Camp: Combine all ingredients in 3-quart pot, adding longer-cooking vegetables first and things like snow peas and bean sprouts only about three minutes before serving. The vegetables should be crunchy.

Miso Soup

Makes 4 servings

Some of the instant miso soups are pretty good, but they can't compare with this. There are many different kinds of miso. I like the tangy Aka, or red miso. You should take care not to boil the soup once you've added the miso paste—the Japanese say it destroys the favorable bacteria and spoils the taste of the soup. This recipe calls for fresh vegetables that keep for up to a week on the trail, but you may substitute dehydrated or freeze-dried vegetables if you wish.

1 medium onion, sliced
2 medium carrots, sliced
1 cup sliced cabbage
1 TB grated fresh ginger
2 TB sesame oil
4 cups water
½ cup miso, or more, depending on the kind you
   use
1 TB Tamari sauce
20 snow peas
½ cup cubed tofu, vacuum-packed

At Home: Pack all vegetables and ginger in separate brown paper bags. Put sesame oil in nalgene bottle or self-sealing packet. Miso can be carried in a ziploc bag.

In Camp: 1. Sauté first 4 vegetables in sesame oil for 5 minutes. Add water and cook till tender, about 10 minutes. 2. Take some of the hot water and thin the miso paste. Gradually add miso to soup pot. Heat through but don't boil. 3. Add Tamari sauce, snow peas and tofu, simmer for 5 minutes more and serve.

Sherried Mushroom Bisque

Makes 6 servings

Sherry, mushrooms, and butter make an exquisite combination in this classic soup.

> 1½ cups sliced dried mushrooms *or* 1 lb fresh
>   mushrooms, sliced
> 1 chicken bouillon cube
> 2 cups water
> 1 small leek or onion, diced *or* 2 TB dried leeks or
>   onions
> 5 TB butter
> 3 TB flour
> 1 cup dried milk mixed with 2 cups water
> salt and pepper
> 1 TB dry sherry

At Home: Put bouillon cube, leek or onion, dried mushrooms and flour in separate packages and put all in a large ziploc along with a small container of sherry. Fresh mushrooms will keep for at least a week if packed in a brown paper bag. Don't wash or cut them and make certain that they're very dry when packed and not crowded together (use 2 or 3 paper bags for a pound).

In Camp: **1.** If you're using dried mushrooms, rehydrate until tender in 2 cups boiling water with bouillon cube. Drain rehydrated mushrooms and reserve liquid. In a skillet, sauté rehydrated mushrooms or fresh sliced mushrooms in 1 TB butter with onions or leeks over medium heat for about 10 minutes. Set aside in covered 3-quart pot. **2.** Make a white sauce: In skillet melt remaining butter, add flour gradually and stir with a whisk until blended. Cook over low heat, stirring constantly, for 10 minutes, then slowly blend in milk mixture and stir till mixture is thickened and smooth. **3.** Combine white sauce with mushrooms in 3-quart pot and add chicken broth mixture. Simmer for about 10 minutes or more, adding more water to thin if necessary. Season with salt and pepper. Stir in sherry about 5 minutes before serving.

15

Dehydrated Main Dishes, Soups, and Jerky

It's fun to prepare and dry your own instant trail meals, and you may be surprised at just how delicious they taste when reconstituted. Cook down liquids as much as possible when cooking main dishes to be dehydrated, use as little oil as possible in their preparation, and make all pieces of vegetables small and the same size so everything will dry properly and uniformly.

Don't use meat in the main dishes you plan to dehydrate. Meat will be better added to the cooking pot later. For example, slice Andouille sausage into the *Cajun Black Beans* in camp. The black beans retain a more distinct flavor of their own, and the sausage will taste fresh and spicy.

These four soup and main-dish recipes can be reconstituted into at least 10 different meals. The *French Onion Soup Base* also makes an outstanding pasta sauce with Parmesan cheese; spaghetti sauce can be a base for soups, pizza, and so on.

These recipes are representative of other old favorites you can turn into quick trail dinners. You may want to try dehydrating your favorite recipe for

164

chili using the black beans recipe as a guide, or perhaps *Curried Lentil Soup* will inspire you to dehydrate your favorite split pea soup recipe.

As noted earlier, the sooner you use these dishes, the better they'll taste. Store in the refrigerator and never attempt to dry main dishes containing cream or eggs. And—just to make sure—use them within a couple of weeks after drying.

Black Beans

Makes 8 servings

After drying, this recipe can be rehydrated into a black-bean soup with a shot of sherry, into a thick refried bean dip, or into Cajun Black Beans *by adding Andouille sausage.*

2 cups black beans
2 or three yellow onions, diced
2 or 3 garlic cloves
2 jalapeño peppers
2 or 3 milder peppers—Anaheim, paprika, or pasilla
2 peppers—red, yellow or green bell, or pimiento
1 tsp salt
¼ tsp pepper
2 tsp ground cumin
1 tsp oregano leaves
olive oil
⅓ cup Marukan seasoned gourmet rice vinegar

At Home: 1. Cover beans with water and soak overnight or for 24 hours, and during this time pour off and replenish bean water several times; this helps prevent flatulence later.

2. Black beans take a long time to cook. Start by cooking them perfectly plain; don't put salt in the water. Simmer partly covered on low heat for at least 5 hours. You don't really need to watch them once you get the heat regulated. You'll get better quality beans if you cook them relatively slowly, don't let them sit and boil. Don't add anything else

until they are cooked through. They should be soft, but not mushy and—this is important—the liquid they're cooking in should be getting thick. When they are soft, take a potato masher and smash some of the beans in the pot. This releases starch and hastens the thickening.

3. When the bean liquor is thick and rich, prepare the other ingredients. (You could also stop here and dry them plain for other bean dishes on the trail to which you'd add spices later.) Cut peppers in half lengthwise. Remove seeds and ribs (this reduces the hotness) and thinly slice horizontally. Sauté in olive oil for 5 minutes with onions. Add garlic and spices and cook a few more minutes. Add this mixture to beans and continue to cook for another hour, adjusting the seasonings as you wish. Because you're going to dry them, they should cook down very thick. About 15 minutes before taking beans off heat, add vinegar.

4. To dehydrate, spread beans evenly on trays and dry at 145 degrees. They should be completely dry. They won't stick together like fruit leather, they'll be separate and they are rather fragile, so avoid crushing them.

5. Package with vacuum packaging machine, with Seal-A-Meal, or in ziplocs and store in refrigerator until ready to use. Two cups when dry weighs 8 oz, and 1¼ cups dried beans makes 1 large backpacker's serving.

In Camp: Rehydrate with ½ to ¾ cup water per 1¼ cups beans, depending on the dish you're making. The beans will rehydrate in 10 to 15 minutes. Heat and serve.

Basic Spaghetti Sauce

Makes 4 servings

This basic tomato sauce can be used in your backpacking menus for all kinds of dishes: pizza toppings, minestrone or other soups, Eggplant Parmesan, and, of course, it's a pasta sauce. Make a big batch of it if you like. If you don't have time to dry it all now, freeze and dehydrate later.

2 yellow onions, chopped
½ cup grated carrot
¼ cup finely chopped celery
Optional: 1 tsp jalapeño pepper, seeded, deveined
    and minced
3 TB chopped garlic
½ tsp leaf oregano
½ tsp sugar
1 6-oz can tomato paste
3 28-oz cans canned tomatoes, drained
20 fresh basil leaves, minced or 1 TB dried basil
4 TB chopped fresh Italian parsley
½ cup red wine
salt and pepper

At Home: 1. Sauté onions till translucent. Add carrot, celery, jalapeño pepper, garlic and sauté for another 2 to 3 minutes. Add oregano and sugar and stir for a minute before adding the tomatoes (don't add their liquid). 2. Cook at simmer for at least 2 hours. Don't let it boil; it should simmer for 2 or 3 hours. When the sauce is thick and rich, add basil, parsley, salt and pepper, and red wine. Simmer for 30 more minutes. 3. To dehydrate, spread sauce on trays. Put in dehydrator or oven at 145 degrees until dry. The dehydrated sauce will be pliable, like fruit leather; remove from plastic tray while still warm. Store in refrigerator.

In Camp: Rehydrate and use as directed in recipes.

French Onion Soup Base

Makes 6 soup servings,
2 to 3 pasta sauce servings

This Fench Onion Soup is the real thing, and it's an outrageously delicious pasta sauce with Parmesan cheese. You could even rehydrate it to a thick spread and eat on bread. I adapted this recipe from Julia Child's "Soupe a l'Oignon" in Mastering the Art of French Cooking. *As she tells us, the onions need long, slow cooking in butter to develop their deep rich flavor.*

5 cups thinly sliced yellow onions
3 TB butter
1 TB olive oil
1 tsp salt
¼ tsp sugar (helps the onions to brown)
3 TB flour
2 cups beef bouillon, boiling
½ cup dry white wine
salt and pepper
Optional: beef bouillon cube

At Home: 1. Cook the onions slowly with butter and oil in a covered, heavy-bottomed saucepan for 15 minutes. 2. Uncover, raise heat to moderate, and stir in salt and sugar. Cook 30 to 40 minutes stirring frequently until the onions are golden brown. They will shrink quite a bit during this time. 3. Sprinkle in the flour and stir for three minutes, then slowly blend in boiling bouillon. This will make a thick sauce. Add wine and season to taste. 4. To dry, spread mixture on drying trays. Dry at 145 degrees until dry. Package and store in refrigerator.

In Camp: Rehydrate with boiling water. Add optional beef bouillon cube if desired and make into soup (4-6 cups of water), or pasta sauce (1-2 cups). *Note:* Because of the high oil content, for best flavor this dish should be dehydrated not more than a week before your camping trip.

Curried Lentil Soup Base

Makes 8 servings

The Indian name for this soup is Dahl Shorba. *It can be made from scratch in camp with the recipe on page 149, or dried at home from this recipe into an instant soup. For a hearty meal, add sliced sausage or fresh vegetables (potatoes, carrots, cauliflower).*

3-4 cups water
2 14½-oz cans chicken broth
2 cups lentils
1 fresh onion
3 cloves garlic
1 TB grated fresh ginger
4 tsp Indian curry powder
2 tsp coriander seeds, crushed
¼ tsp red pepper flakes
1 TB olive oil

At Home: 1. Combine water, chicken broth cubes, and lentils. Bring to boil, reduce heat, and cover. Simmer on low heat for 20 to 45 minutes or until lentils are cooked through; it won't take long if you use orange or yellow lentils. Keep watching it—if it thickens too much you may have to add more water, but add as little as possible. 2. Dice onion, mince garlic and cook and stir them in oil together with curry, coriander seeds (crush with back of cooking spoon) and red peppers over medium heat for 7 minutes. Stir spice mixture into lentils. Cover. Cook over medium-low heat for 20 minutes. Cook down to a thick paste, taking care not to burn while it's cooking down. 3. Spread on plastic sheets in dryer. Dry at 145 degrees until dry, about 6 hours. Repackage and store in refrigerator until ready to use.

In Camp: Rehydrate with boiling water, heat, add water until desired thickness and serve.

Making Jerky

Making jerky—meat, poultry, or fish—is an uncomplicated three-step process:

- Thinly slice meat.

- Marinate for a few hours.

- Place in dehydrator (or oven) until dry.

Use low-fat cuts of meat, fish, or poultry. Lamb and fresh pork are too fatty; venison and elk make excellent jerky.

The marinades below are of two types: dry-cure and wet. Use a glass, plastic, stoneware or stainless steel container for your marinade. You need a certain amount of salt to guard against spoilage, but too much makes the meat inedible. I tried some old-time recipes using heavily salted brines, and the results were terrible. Liquid smoke added to marinades imparts a pleasing smoked taste to dried meats, poultry, and fish; it can be found in supermarkets. Use it sparingly! It's awfully strong, and you should use less for fish than for beef. Cover the marinade dish tightly, or your refrigerator will smell like liquid smoke for days.

Follow the guidelines for drying other foods: Cut into uniform sizes, and don't crowd in the dryer or oven. As the jerky dries, beads of oil may come to the surface; pat it dry with paper towels. It's essential that the initial drying temperature be at least 140 degrees to guard against spoilage. Be especially careful not to over-dry jerky. You certainly want it to be dry enough to be safe, but it's a disappointing waste of time and money to dry it to the tooth shattering stage. Remember, fish and turkey are more delicate than beef jerky and take far less time to dry. Jerky is dry enough if it cracks when you bend it, but isn't so brittle that it breaks in two. To keep jerky at peak flavor, store it in the refrigerator.

Beef Jerky

Use round steak, flank steak, top sirloin, or some other low-fat cut of beef. To slice, use a very sharp knife; some people partly freeze the meat first to make cutting easier. Cut in strips 3 inches or longer by about 1-inch wide and ¼-inch thick. Cut across the grain for more tender jerky, with the grain for tougher, chewy strips. Some people like to cut jerky in paper thin sheets.

Drying Jerky After marinating or dry-curing jerky according to directions in the recipes below, dry in your dehydrator at 140 to 160 degrees for the first 4 hours, then you may reduce heat to 130 degrees until dry. For oven drying, heat should be 140 to 160 degrees for about 8 hours, then lower to 130 degrees till dry. I've dried jerky in the oven at a constant temperature of 150 degrees for ten hours. It works, but you'll get better results with a dehydrator, and also by starting with a higher temperature and then lowering it.

Camper's Classic Jerky Marinade
Makes about ½ lb jerky

1 tsp salt
1 tsp pepper
3 TB brown sugar
¼ cup Worcestershire sauce
¼ cup Tamari or soy sauce
1 TB liquid smoke
2 lbs round or flank steak or other low-fat cut of meat, sliced

1. In a bowl, mix together marinade ingredients. 2. Pour over meat slices; thoroughly wet all sides of meat with marinade and layer in the marinating dish. 3. Cover tightly and marinate in refrigerator overnight or from 6 to 12 hours. For best results rotate meat layers every couple of hours until ready to dry. Dry according to above directions.

Ginger Jerky Marinade
Makes about ½ lb jerky

½ tsp salt
½ tsp pepper
½ tsp ground ginger
1 TB fresh ginger
1 large clove garlic, minced
½ cup soy sauce
¼ cup sugar
2 lbs round or flank steak or other cut of sliced meat

Follow the directions for *Camper's Classic Jerky*.

Dry-Cure Curry Jerky
Makes about ½ lb jerky

1 tsp salt
¼ tsp pepper
3 big pinches of cinnamon
3 big pinches of ground cloves
1 tsp cumin seeds, crushed
½ tsp ground cumin
1 TB curry powder
1 tsp ground ginger
1-2 cloves garlic, minced
2 lbs round or flank steak or other cut of sliced meat

1. Combine ingredients and thoroughly mix together. **2.** Add meat slices and work spices into grain of meat. **3.** Layer meat in the dish, cover tightly and marinate in the refrigerator overnight or 6 to 12 hours. Dry according to above directions.

Dry-Cure Southwest Jerky
Makes about ½ lb jerky

1 tsp salt
1 tsp pepper
¼-½ tsp cayenne
3 TB chili powder
2 tsp cumin
2 cloves garlic, minced
3 TB fresh cilantro, minced
2 lbs round or flank steak or other cut of sliced meat

Follow the directions for *Dry-Cure Curry Jerky*.

Hamburger Jerky

Buy the leanest grade of hamburger you can find. I usually mix about ½ cup of teriyaki or soy sauce with 2 pounds of hamburger and dry at 145 degrees for about 6 hours until it's crispy dry. Be sure to pat extra oil away with a paper towel during the drying process. You can also substitute hamburger for the steak or sliced meat in the dry-cure jerky recipes, or use about half of the wet marinade for 2 pounds of hamburger.

Smoked Teriyaki Turkey Jerky

Makes about ¼ lb jerky

Turkey jerky is special—and at health-food stores it costs $25 a pound. It's best sliced in paper thin sheets. You can buy a whole turkey, but I think it's best to buy just a turkey breast or turkey thighs. Buying turkey cutlets saves you some hassle but it's a relatively expensive way to go.

½ **cup soy sauce**
4 TB sugar
2 tsp fresh grated ginger
1 clove garlic, minced
1 TB liquid smoke
3 lbs turkey

1. Cut the raw meat into thin sheets with a very sharp knife. **2.** Mix together the marinade ingredients, pour over the meat and marinate for 3 to 8 hours in the refrigerator. **3.** Dry at 145 degrees for 2 hours, then drop temperature to 130 degrees. Because the meat is so thinly sliced it dries quickly, sticks and tears apart easily if you don't turn it often. If you have a dehydrator, use the plastic screen tray to help with the sticking problem.

Fish Jerky   You can use red snapper, sea bass, swordfish, or any firm fish for fish jerky. Salmon and tuna are outstanding.

Smoked Salmon Jerky
Makes about ½ lb jerky

½ **cup soy sauce**
2 tsp liquid smoke
2 lbs salmon

1. Cut fish into thin strips about ¼" thick, 1-2" wide, and 3-5" long. **2.** Mix together marinade ingredients, pour over fish and marinate for about 6 hours. **3.** Dry at 145 degrees for 2 hours, then lower temperature to 130 degrees until dry. Salmon will bead oil during drying, so be sure to keep soaking up oil with a paper towel.

Teriyaki Tuna Jerky
Makes about ½ lb jerky

½ **cup soy sauce**
4 TB sugar
2 tsp grated fresh ginger
1 clove garlic, minced *or* **about ¾ cup of your favorite commercial teriyaki sauce**
2 lbs fresh raw tuna

Follow the directions for *Smoked Salmon Jerky*.

16

Dinners

These dinner recipes run the gamut from gourmet to simple and traditional. Some are easy one-pot meals and others consist of several courses. There are Spartan meals to cook at high altitude and elegant celebration dinners. A Japanese sushi buffet, *Eggplant Parmesan, Shrimp Steamed in Beer,* and *Thai Peanut Chicken* are among these thirty-five dinner recipes. There should be something for everyone here.

Szechuan Snow Peas

Makes 4 servings

This is a quick and delicious meal, just the thing for one of those evenings when you get into camp much later than expected. All the preparation is done at home; in camp you simply cook pasta or rice and add the sauce. And snow peas keep for a long time when properly packaged. I've eaten them on the sixth day out—what a treat it is to have a crisp, green vegetable after many days on the trail.

12 oz pasta or Minute Rice
2-4 dozen snow peas

Peanut Sauce:

½ **cup hot water**
½ **cup smooth peanut butter**
3 tsp soy sauce
2 TB Marukan seasoned gourmet rice vinegar *or* **1**
    TB white wine vinegar
1 green onion, finely chopped
2 cloves finely minced garlic
1 tsp sugar
¼ **tsp red pepper flakes**
Garnishes: fresh cilantro or *Cilantro-Peanut Oil*
    Pesto **(page 179), 1 green onion, minced,**
    fresh or dried

At Home: 1. In a mixing bowl blend water and peanut butter until creamy. Stir in soy, rice vinegar, garlic, sugar, and red pepper flakes. **2.** Put peanut sauce in a small nalgene bottle. Package rice or fettucini in ziploc bag. In separate brown paper bags put snow peas, cilantro, and green onion.

In Camp: 1. Start heating water for rice or pasta. While it's heating trim ends off snow peas. If you're cooking pasta, add snow peas about three minutes before it's done. If cooking rice, stir in snow peas with fork five minutes before serving. The snow peas should be cooked, but slightly crunchy. **2.** Toss peanut sauce with hot pasta or rice and snow peas. Garnish with cilantro or pesto, and green onion.

Pesto

I serve a pesto on nearly every wilderness trip I have. I think pesto is the world's best backpacking food because it's ready to eat, it's concentrated, it keeps for days if kept in a cool place in your pack— and garlic is reputed to be a natural mosquito repellent!

Pestos are usually a blend of herbs, oil, cheese and garlic. It's most often eaten with pasta, but you can add pesto to soup, use it like butter on baked potatoes, and spread it on bread or crackers. Some pesto addicts even eat it on scrambled eggs at breakfast. Pesto can be used in cooking to give your recipe a fresh herb taste, and it can disguise the rather processed taste of some commercial packaged soups and freeze-dried dinners.

Pesto keeps well in the freezer, so you may want to make a large supply to keep on hand. If you don't want to make your own, you can find freshly made basil pesto in a good delicatessen. The gourmet section of fancy supermarkets often has pretty good pesto sold in glass jars. Whatever you do— *don't* get powdered pesto mix—it's an abomination.

Basil Pesto

Makes about 1½ cups

Basil pesto is the original, classic dish which originated in Genoa, Italy. You can vary the ingredients in pesto, such as substituting macadamia nuts or walnuts for pine nuts or omitting butter or Romano cheese. You'll still get a good-tasting pesto—but be sure to use only fresh garlic, fresh basil, and real olive oil.

2 cups fresh basil leaves
⅓-½ cup olive oil
2 TB pine nuts
2-4 cloves garlic
1 tsp salt
¼ tsp pepper
2 TB butter softened to room temperature
⅓ cup freshly grated Parmesan cheese
2 TB freshly grated Romano cheese

At Home:

1. Remove basil leaves from the stems and set aside (discard the stems). 2. Put half the olive oil, nuts, garlic, salt, pepper and butter in a food processor or blender and mix at high speed until evenly blended. Add basil leaves and remainder of oil and mix. Stop often and with a rubber spatula scrape down the sides of food processor till everything is evenly blended. You want basil leaves to be well-blended into the other ingredients, but don't over-blend to a green liquid; some tiny pieces of the leaves should be recognizable. 3. Add Parmesan and Romano cheeses and mix until just blended. The finished product should be pasty—about the consistency of oatmeal. 4. Package in a nalgene bottle, and twist the lid firmly closed.

In Camp:

Cook pasta of your choice and mix pesto into steaming hot pasta, or serve plain pasta and pass the pesto jar. Two tablespoons is a conservative estimate for one serving; most people want more. Serve with additional Parmesan cheese if desired.

Variation: If you can't get fresh basil, try *Parsley Pesto*. Substitute parsley for basil and use flat-leaf Italian parsley if possible.

South of the Border Pesto

Makes about 1½ cups

Serve this over cilantro-corn ribbon pasta or corn elbow macaroni or spread on a warm tortilla.

½ cup olive oil
⅓ cup pistachio nuts
2-4 cloves garlic
½ tsp salt
¼ tsp pepper
dash Tabasco sauce
2 cups loosely packed cilantro with stems, cleaned
  and thoroughly dried
½ cup Monterey Jack cheese, finely grated

At Home: Cut cilantro in about 2" lengths and set aside. Then follow general directions for making *Basil Pesto* from step 2 except stir in the grated jack cheese by hand after pesto is made.

Cilantro-Peanut Oil Pesto

Makes about 1 cup

Use a high-quality, fragrant cold-pressed peanut oil for this recipe. Stir into Thai Tom Yum Soup, use in Mexican or Chinese food—or for a surprisingly delicious treat, put on baked or hash-brown sweet potatoes.

⅓ cup peanut oil
2 cups loosely packed cilantro with stems, cleaned
  and thoroughly dried
scant ½ tsp salt
¼ tsp pepper

At Home: **1.** Put oil, salt, and pepper into food processor or blender. Pulse once to mix. Add cilantro and pulse processor blade until cilantro is finely chopped but not pulverized to a liquid. **2.** Package in a nalgene bottle.

12,000' Oriental Stir-Fry

Makes 4 servings

This is the meal I usually serve to my group the night before we climb Mt. Whitney at the end of a 13-mile day. Serve with instant miso soup and Minute Rice; hot chocolate and fortune cookies for dessert.

A selection of freeze-dried or dehydrated veggies
to equal about 5 oz, such as:
 bell peppers
 mushrooms
 peas
 green beans
 corn
1 small onion, diced
1 TB fresh grated ginger
2 garlic cloves, minced
2 TB safflower oil
2 TB sesame oil
Optional: 1 small can of Oriental veggies: bamboo
 shoots *or* water chestnuts *or* bean sprouts
⅓ cup cashews
24 snow peas
1 8-oz package of vacuum-packaged tofu, cut in
 squares
soy sauce

At Home:
Put all freeze-dried or dehydrated vegetables together in a boilable plastic bag. Pack cans and vacuum-packed tofu. Pack produce in brown paper bags. Bring a small nalgene bottle of soy sauce. Mix oils and carry in a nalgene bottle. Package cashews in plastic bag.

In Camp:
1. Rehydrate vegetables. 2. Sauté onion, garlic, and ginger in oil. Add rehydrated vegetables and canned vegetables and cook for about 5 minutes. Add cashews and snow peas. 3. When snow peas are almost cooked, add tofu and gently stir in and heat through. Sprinkle with soy sauce and serve.

Alsatian Cabbage

Makes 4 servings

Dried cabbage? If you really don't like cabbage skip this recipe—but it's surprisingly good. It's inspired by a recipe from Julia Child's Mastering the Art of French Cooking *and is especially good when the weather turns cold. This dish isn't exactly "Choucroute Braisee à l'Alsacienne," but it's full of country flavors and will warm and sustain you through a cold night in the mountains.*

3 oz (approximately 3 cups) dried cabbage
½ cup thinly sliced carrots *or* ¼ cup dried carrots
⅓ cup dried leeks *or* onions
2 cooked potatoes, cubed *or* 5 oz dried potatoes
1-2 TB butter
1 Polish sausage *or* apple-chicken sausage *or* ¼ lb
    ham
¼ tsp caraway seeds
1 chicken bouillon cube
1 cup white wine *or* ¼ cup gin

At Home: Package together in a ziploc the dried vegetables. Package sausage and fresh vegetables in separate brown paper bags. Put caraway seeds and bouillon cube in a small plastic bag and carry wine or gin in a small nalgene bottle. Include butter with your main supply.

In Camp: 1. When you get into camp rehydrate vegetables with water to cover for at least 15 minutes. 2. When the vegetables are ready, melt butter in frying pan and over medium-high heat sauté sausage or ham with caraway seeds for 3-5 minutes. Then add vegetables and sauté for 10 minutes. 3. Add wine or gin and chicken bouillon cube. Cover and simmer for 15 minutes, stirring occasionally. Prepare this dish ahead of time if you wish—the longer it sits, the better it tastes. This goes well with hearty dark rye bread and stewed apples with cinnamon for dessert.

Herbed Sun-Dried Tomatoes in Olive Oil

Makes 2 cups

In a gourmet shop you'll pay around $12 for an 8-oz jar of sun-dried tomatoes packed in olive oil, and several people have told me that these are the best sun-dried tomatoes they've ever eaten. Spread on French bread and eat with feta, goat cheese, or just plain lettuce. You could easily make this in camp, too.

1½ cups sun-dried tomatoes
¾ cup olive oil
15-20 cloves garlic, peeled
½ tsp paprika
½ tsp oregano
1 tsp ground coriander
½ tsp salt
10 whole peppercorns
⅓ cup Marukan seasoned gourmet rice vinegar
2 TB basalmic vinegar

At Home: 1. Rehydrate tomatoes with boiling water to cover. When rehydrated, drain and gently squeeze out excess water. **2.** While tomatoes are rehydrating, gently sauté peeled whole garlic cloves in olive oil at a very low heat for about 15 minutes or more. The garlic should get soft and spreadable. This may seem like a lot of garlic, but when cooked in this way it becomes very mild. **3.** When garlic is soft, stir in spices, salt and peppercorns and cook for 5 more minutes. **4.** Add vinegars and rehydrated tomatoes and cook for another few minutes. Spoon into a nalgene wide mouth bottle and let cool. If kept in a cool place in your pack, these tomatoes will keep for several days.

Good Old Macaroni and Cheese

Makes 3 servings

Use a good, sharp cheddar here such as aged New York cheddar or Rabbit cheese.

2 TB butter
½ cup onion, minced
1½ cups or more of sharp cheddar cheese, grated
¼ cup ground Parmesan cheese
½ cup dry milk mixed with 1 cup water
8 oz macaroni

At Home: Wrap cheddar in brown paper. Put Parmesan and dry milk in separate ziplocs. Add butter and onion to main supply. Package macaroni and pack in cooking pot so it won't get crushed.

In Camp: 1. Sauté onion in butter for 5 minutes. 2. Prepare macaroni as directed. When macaroni is cooked, drain and add butter and onion and stir well. Stir in cheddar, Parmesan cheese and milk. Heat through till cheese is melted.

Variation: Add a can of tuna and sprinkle with parsley. Some people like macaroni and cheese with a dash of Tabasco sauce.

Burr's Seafood

Makes 4 servings

Burr cringes at the thought of this dish being made with powdered milk instead of real cream, but it's still delicious and using dry milk means you can enjoy this exquisite meal several days down the trail.

10 cloves garlic, minced
3 TB butter
6-½ oz can crab
10-oz can whole baby clams
½ bunch fresh flat-leaf Italian minced parsley
  ***or* 2 TB dehydrated parsley**
½ stick butter
½ cup dry milk mixed with water to make 1 cup
¼ cup dry sherry
Parmesan cheese
12-16 oz pasta

At Home:

Package parsley in brown paper bag. Add garlic, butter and dry milk to main supply. Put sherry in nalgene bottle. Pack cans.

In Camp:

1. Gently sauté garlic in butter at low heat for about 10 minutes. Drain seafood and reserve clam liquor. Add canned seafood and gently warm through. Stir in parsley. **2.** Add milk and clam liquor and cook for 5 minutes. Set aside in a warm place while you cook pasta. **3.** About 5-10 minutes before serving stir sherry into sauce. The moment pasta is drained, add sauce and toss and serve immediately with Parmesan cheese if desired.

Mexican Chicken Tostadas

Makes 6 servings

You can have a huge Mexican Fiesta dinner after several days on the trail. Everything here will keep that long, even fresh cabbage. Buy the avocados as hard as baseballs and take care to pack them in a cooking pot to keep them from getting crushed as they ripen.

1 jalapeño pepper
2 red bell peppers, cut in strips and dehydrated
1 tsp cumin
½ tsp oregano
12½-oz can chicken
oil
tostada makings such as:
   cabbage (fresh or dehydrated) *or* iceberg lettuce
   avocados
   fresh onion
7-oz can salsa
dry jack cheese
12 flat, crisp tortilla shells

At Home: Package cheese and fresh vegetables in brown paper bags. Put dehydrated vegetables in boilable plastic bags. Pack cans. Make a spice packet for cumin and oregano. Add oil to main supply.

In Camp: 1. Mince jalapeño pepper and sauté in oil with spices and dehydrated peppers for 5 minutes. Stir in chicken, warm through and set aside while tostada makings are being prepared. 2. Shred fresh cabbage or lettuce. Slice avocados. Mince ½ cup fresh onion. Grate cheese and open salsa can. Set out tostada shells. Serve this Mexican feast with rice, *Refried Bean Dip* and *Mexican Fondue* (see next 2 recipes) if you wish.

Refried Bean Dip

Appetizer for 6 people

7 oz package Fantastic Foods Refried Bean Mix *or*
7 oz dehydrated pinto beans
4 oz dry jack cheese, grated
7 oz can salsa
12 flat, crisp tortilla shells broken into chip size

At Home: Remove bean mix from box, repackage in plastic bag and include directions. Package dry jack in brown paper bag. Pack salsa can.

In Camp: **1.** In a pot with a lid, prepare bean mix with boiling water as directed or pour 2 cups water over dehydrated beans. **2.** Grate cheese and stir into beans, reserving some for garnish. **3.** Pour salsa over beans, top with remaining cheese and put lid on pot till cheese is melted. **4.** Serve with tortillas. This bean dip is also great in tostadas or tortillas.

Mexican Fondue

Makes 8 servings, more if an appetizer

1 small onion, minced
4 TB butter
16 oz can chopped tomatoes
4 oz can chopped green chilies
16 oz Monterey Jack, grated
1 TB cornstarch
salt to taste
⅓ cup dry milk mixed with ¾ cup water
12 flat, crisp tortilla shells broken into chip size

At Home: If you're going to be eating this the first or second night, grate cheese and toss with cornstarch to coat and package in plastic bag. Otherwise, pack cheese ungrated, put cornstarch in a plastic film can and grate and toss with cornstarch in camp. Package onion in brown paper bag. Add butter and dry milk to main supply. Pack canned goods.

In Camp: **1.** Sauté onion in butter till translucent. **2.** Add tomatoes and chilies and simmer for 15 minutes. Add grated cheese (combine with cornstarch if grated in camp). When cheese begins to melt, gradually add milk. You may not have to add it all. **3.** Break up flat tortilla shells and dip into *Mexican Fondue.*

Sherried Mushrooms and Sweet Peppers

Makes 4 servings

This is good with any pasta or grain—and great over Fantastic Foods' Nature's Burgers.

> ¾ cup dehydrated sliced mushrooms, (use regular market mushrooms or better yet, try chanterelles or morels)
> 5-7 dried sweet red, green and yellow peppers
> 2 cloves garlic
> olive oil
> 1-2 TB butter
> ½ cup dry milk
> 1 cup water
> 2 TB dry sherry
> Optional: grated Parmesan cheese

At Home: Package peppers and mushrooms in separate ziplocs. Include garlic, olive oil and butter with main supply. Put sherry in a nalgene bottle. Put dry milk and Parmesan cheese in separate ziploc bags.

In Camp: **1.** Rehydrate mushrooms and peppers in boiling water to cover. This will take 10-15 minutes. When veggies are rehydrated pour off water, gently press out excess water, and reserve this liquid for sauce. **2.** In a frying pan sauté peppers, mushrooms, and sliced garlic cloves in olive oil for about 7 minutes at medium heat. **3.** Add butter and turn down heat; stir in dry milk mixed with 1 cup water till warmed through. You will have a rich, reddish brown sauce; the sauce will probably need thinning so add reserved rehydrating liquid a little at a time. Remove from heat and stir in sherry. Cover and set aside in a warm place till pasta, grain or Nature's Burgers are ready to eat.

Polenta Pesto with Gorgonzola Cheese
Makes 4 servings

This gourmet dish is fast and simple. Use a good, aged Gorgonzola, serve with French bread or bread sticks.

1½ cups instant polenta
½ cup *Basil Pesto* **(page 178)**
4 oz Gorgonzola
salt and pepper

At Home: Package instant polenta in sealable plastic bag. Make *Basil Pesto* and put in nalgene bottle. Wrap Gorgonzola in brown paper (not plastic wrap) if it must keep for a few days.

In Camp: **1.** Make instant polenta according to package directions. It should take only about 5 minutes to cook. **2.** When polenta is ready, remove from heat and make a shallow well in the center. Fill well with pesto. Crumble Gorgonzola over all and put lid back on pot until cheese melts a bit and its strong flavor is released, about 5 minutes.

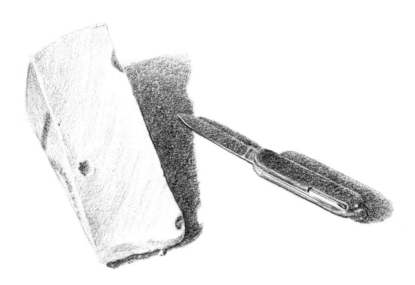

Eggplant Parmesan
Makes 8 servings
A special dish well worth the extra effort.

**2 medium eggplants, cut in rounds and dehydrated
olive oil
6 garlic cloves
1 small yellow onion, diced
2 tsp leaf oregano
1 tsp dried basil
2 tubes concentrated Italian tomato paste and 1
cup sun-dried tomatoes** *or* **2 6-oz cans tomato
paste and 2 11-oz cans cut-up tomatoes** *or* **8 oz
dehydrated** *Basic Spaghetti Sauce* **(page 167)
rehydrated with 2-3 cups water
2 TB brandy
12 oz Mozzarella cheese
4 oz Parmesan cheese
½ bunch fresh parsley, preferably the flat-leaf
Italian style** *or* **⅓ cup dehydrated parsley**

At Home: Package dehydrated foods in separate ziplocs or boilable plastic bags. Pack canned tomatoes and tomato paste. Make a spice packet with oregano and basil. Put brandy in nalgene bottle. Wrap Mozzarella in brown paper (not plastic wrap). Parmesan can go in a ziploc. Add olive oil to main supply.

In Camp: 1. Rehydrate dried foods for about 15 minutes. Press excess liquid out of eggplant and sauté in olive oil for 10 minutes. Cover and set aside. 2. Prepare tomato sauce: Sauté onion, garlic, pepper, basil and oregano in olive oil for 5-7 minutes. Add rehydrated *Basic Spaghetti Sauce* or other tomatoes. Simmer about 15 minutes. Stir in brandy. Cook 5 minutes longer. 3. Thickly coat Banks Frybake Pan (or other cooking pot) with olive oil. Then add ingredients in layers starting with a layer of tomato sauce, then a layer of eggplant, a layer of Italian parsley, Mozzarella and Parmesan cheeses. Repeat till pan is full, finishing layers with tomato sauce. Sprinkle Parmesan on top. 4. For best results, bake in a mini-oven such as Banks Frybake Pan with stove on simmer and a small twig fire on top to make coals for 15-30 minutes. You may also use a cooking pot set on a heat diffuser with stove on simmer; check often to prevent burning on bottom. When ready to eat, your *Eggplant Parmesan* will be a steaming, bubbling masterpiece, thick with melted cheese.

Andouille and Summer Garden Stew with Polenta

Makes 6 servings

Polenta and sausages are a classic combination in Italian cuisine and oh-so-wonderful. I've made this dish the fifth day on the trail at 10,500 feet—and it was devoured by hungry hikers.

Summer garden vegetables such as:
   2 medium zucchini
   2 medium yellow summer squash
   3 red, yellow, and/or green bell peppers, cut in strips and dehydrated
   1 medium eggplant, cut in rounds, then ½" strips and dehydrated
½ Andouille Sausage (about 6 oz)
6 oz dehydrated *Basic Spaghetti Sauce* (page 167) , rehydrate with 2-3 cups water) *or* 1 6-oz can tomato paste and ½ cup tomato flakes plus 2-3 cups water
1 small onion, diced
Optional: ½ cup red wine *or* ¼ cup brandy
1 cup *Basil Pesto* (page 178)
⅔ cup Parmesan cheese
2 cups instant polenta

At Home: Package dehydrated foods in separate boilable plastic bags. Package fresh vegetables in brown paper bags. Put pesto and wine or brandy in separate nalgene bottles. Package Parmesan cheese in ziploc bag.

In Camp: 1. Rehydrate dried foods in their boilable plastic bags. 2. Cut sausage in ¼" rounds and sauté in frying pan. Add onion to sausage and cook till translucent. 3. Add rehydrated *Basic Spaghetti Sauce* or tomato paste and tomato flakes plus 2-3 cups water. Simmer 5 minutes. Add rehydrated vegetables and wine or brandy and cook for 15 more minutes. **3.** While tomato sauce is cooking, slice fresh veggies as if for stir-fry. Thickly coat Banks Frybake Pan (or other cooking pot) with olive oil. Then add ingredients in layers starting with a layer of tomato sauce, then a layer of fresh veggies, a layer of pesto, and a layer of Parmesan cheese. Repeat till pan is full, finishing layers with tomato sauce. Sprinkle Parmesan cheese on top. **4.** Bake in Banks Frybake Pan with stove on simmer and a small twig fire on top to make coals for 15-30 minutes. You may also use a cooking pot set on a heat diffuser with stove on simmer; check often to prevent burning on bottom. **5.** Prepare instant polenta as directed. When cooked, pour polenta on individual plates. Make a well in the center and spoon in sausage and vegetables. Eat while steaming hot.

Pasta with Andouille and Fried Sage

Makes 4-6 servings

Bruce Aidell, author of Hot Links and Country Flavors, *contributed this simple and elegant pasta recipe.*

½ **lb Andouille sausage**
½ **cup olive oil**
1 cup loosely packed fresh sage leaves
1 lb pasta of your choice
grated Parmesan cheese

At Home: Wrap Andouille sausage in butcher paper or brown paper bag. Add olive oil to main supply. Package fresh sage in brown paper bag. Put Parmesan cheese in a ziploc. Pack pasta inside cooking pots to keep it from getting crushed.

In Camp: **1.** Dice sausage and sauté 5 minutes to render fat. Set aside. **2.** In clean pan, fry sage leaves in hot olive oil for about 1 minute or until crisp. **3.** Prepare pasta. Add sausage and toss immediately with freshly cooked pasta and Parmesan cheese.

Indian Sambaar Stew

Makes 4 servings

This savory brown lentil stew uses home-dried lentils, and is ready to eat in about 15 minutes. Don't hesitate to add fresh vegetables to this recipe. Mixed vegetable lentil stews like this one are common in India, and are usually eaten accompanied by rice and ghee (clarified butter). Buttered Basmati rice would make this flavorful dish a complete meal and add to its complementary protein value.

1 small onion, diced *or* 2 TB dried onion
1 garlic clove, minced
2 tsp fresh ginger (or add 1 tsp powdered ginger to
    spice mixture)
1 jalapeño pepper, seeded, deveined, and minced
    or add ⅛ -¼ tsp cayenne pepper to spice mixture
1 TB butter or oil
½ bar S&B Golden Curry Sauce Mix (3.8-oz pack-
    age) *or:*
    2 TB curry powder, 2 TB whole wheat flour,
    1 tsp turmeric, 1 tsp cumin, pinch cinnamon,
    1 beef bouillon cube
1 cup (3½ oz) dehydrated cooked lentils
½ cup mixed, dried veggies: carrots, celery, red or
    green peppers
¼ cup freeze-dried snow peas
½ cup dried potatoes *or* 2 small baked potatoes
4-5 cups water
salt and pepper

At Home: Put onion, garlic, ginger, and jalapeño pepper (if used) in a paper bag and label. Combine spices, flour, and bouillon cubes and package together. Include butter or oil with main supply. Dried lentils and other vegetables go in sealable plastic bags.

In Camp: 1. Combine 2 cups water, dried vegetables and lentils in 3-quart pot. Bring to a boil, cover and simmer till rehydrated. 2. Add butter, onions, garlic, spices to lentils and vegetables. Cook for 10 minutes. Add any fresh vegetables you're using and slowly add 2 cups water or to desired thickness, simmer for 10 minutes and serve.

Swedish Sailor's Beans

Makes 6 servings

This recipe was given to me by a Swedish sailor. Anders says that in Sweden you can get white beans canned in tomato sauce; in the U.S. he makes do with Van Kamps pork and beans. The cans make it a bit heavy, but it's perfect for a fast and hearty first night meal on a short trip when you don't have much time for pre-trip prep.

½ lb hamburger
1 medium onion, chopped
2 cloves garlic
1 bell pepper, diced
10 mushrooms, sliced
salt and pepper
Optional: 1 or 2 jalapeño or other hot peppers
14½-oz can pork and beans
14½-oz can crushed tomatoes with juice
1 can cream mushroom soup *or* 1 package (one that
    makes 4 cups soup) dehydrated cream of
    mushroom soup mix plus ½ cup water

At Home: Package pepper, mushrooms, garlic and onion in brown paper bags. Insulate hamburger in a layer of newspaper and keep chilled till you get to the trailhead.

In Camp: 1. Sauté hamburger chopped onion, black pepper, garlic, bell pepper, mushrooms and jalapeño peppers (if used) for 10 minutes. 2. Add canned beans, tomatoes, and soup and heat through. Add salt if needed, but the canned things are already salty.

French Onion Fettucini

Makes 3 servings

1 recipe *French Onion Soup Base* (page 168),
  dehydrated or fresh
1-2 cups boiling water
6-8 oz fettucini (or other pasta)
⅓ cup Parmesan cheese

At Home: Package *French Onion Soup Base* in boilable plastic bag. Package Parmesan and pasta in separate ziplocs.

In Camp: 1. Rehydrate *French Onion Soup Base* with boiling water to desired thickness and heat through. 2. Prepare pasta. The moment pasta is drained, add sauce, toss and serve immediately with Parmesan cheese.

Black Bean Polenta Pie

Makes 4 servings

16 oz dehydrated *Black Beans* (page 165) *or* 7-oz
  package Fantastic Foods black bean mix
1 cup polenta
salt and pepper
Optional spices to taste: cumin, garlic, dash
  Tabasco sauce

At Home: Package dehydrated beans and polenta in separate ziploc or Seal-A-Meal bags. Add spices to main supply.

In Camp: 1. Rehydrate home-dried beans with approximately 1½ cups boiling water or prepare bean mix as directed; add water gradually taking care not to make too thin. 2. Heat rehydrated beans in frying pan or Banks Frybake Pan. Adjust seasoning with optional spices if desired. 3. Meanwhile, in a cooking pot prepare polenta according to directions. Let polenta sit for a bit and thicken. Then carefully pour polenta onto the surface of beans in the frying pan to form a crust. Heat through and serve with tortillas or bread.

White Clam Sauce

Makes 3 servings

¼ cup minced onion
¼ cup olive oil
2 garlic cloves, minced
1 tsp thyme
1 TB dehydrated parsley *or* ¼ cup fresh parsley
⅓ cup white wine
10-oz can whole baby clams with their juice
2 Tb butter
3 Tb ground Parmesan cheese plus Parmesan for
    garnish
8 oz pasta (linguini, spaghetti, Angel hair would
    be good choices)

At Home: Pack canned clams. Put a small onion and fresh parsley in brown paper bags. Put thyme (and dried parsley if you're using it) in film can. Put wine in nalgene bottle. Add butter to main supply. Package Parmesan cheese in ziploc bag.

In Camp: **1.** Mince ¼ cup onion and in a frying pan sauté in olive oil till translucent. Mince garlic and saute with onion for another minute. Add thyme, parsley and wine and cook for 5 minutes. **2.** Stir in clams and their juice and warm through. Stir in butter and Parmesan cheese. **3.** Cover and keep in a warm place while you prepare pasta. The moment pasta is drained, add sauce and toss and serve immediately with more cheese.

Near-East Far-Out Bulgur Chicken Pilaf

Makes 6 servings

This pilaf is a meal in itself, but if you want to make it a dinner occasion serve with a red cabbage salad, hummus, pita bread; halvah and hot chocolate for dessert.

¼ cup grated dehydrated carrots
½ tsp dehydrated celery
¼ cup freeze dried peas
1 bell pepper, cut in strips and dehydrated *or* 1
    fresh bell pepper cut in strips
1 TB butter
2 TB olive oil
1 small onion, diced
3 garlic cloves, minced
1½ cups bulgur
spices:
    1 tsp cumin
    ½ tsp turmeric
    1 tsp oregano
    ½ tsp cinnamon
2 TB pine nuts
⅓ cup raisins
2 5-oz cans chicken
2 cups boiling water
24 or more fresh snow peas
Optional: 1 cooked potato
salt and pepper

At Home: Package bulgur in a ziploc. Add butter to main supply. Make a packet of the spices. Package pine nuts and raisins together. Package all dried vegetables together in a boilable plastic bag. Put fresh produce in brown paper bags.

In Camp: 1. Rehydrate vegetables. 2. Heat butter and olive oil in skillet. Add diced onion and garlic, and sauté till onion is translucent. Add bulgur and sauté on medium heat until golden, about 10 minutes. 3. Add spices and cook for 5 minutes more. Add rehydrated vegetables, pine nuts, raisins and one can chicken. Add boiling water and cook on medium heat for 15 minutes or until water is absorbed and bulgur is tender. Add vegetable hydrating water if more water is needed. **4.** Gently stir in the other can of chicken, snow peas, and potato. Salt and pepper to taste. Heat till snow peas are cooked yet slightly crunchy and serve.

Sushi Smorgasbord
Makes 10 servings

People on my trips can hardly believe it when I serve them sushi in the wilderness. It's a completely unexpected treat and these smorgasbord-style dinners are always fun. This is an easy dinner for the cook. Everyone helps slice and dice the sushi makings and diners create their own sushi combinations. This menu was inspired by my Kauai friend John Ono who sends me sun-dried Ahi (tuna) and smoked marlin he makes himself. You may not have a Hawaiian connection for home-smoked fish, but you can get canned gourmet fish at fancy supermarkets.

> 2 cups short-grain rice (try sushi rice if you can
> find it—it's stickier)
> 4 cups water
> ½ cup Marukan seasoned gourmet rice vinegar
> nori (seaweed), for wrapping sushi (I get Nagai's
> Teriyaki Nori in 1½" x 4" size.)
> fish suggestions:
> fresh raw sashimi *or* smoked salmon from the
> deli if you're having this the first night
> smoked marlin or other smoked fish
> canned specialty fish: squid in red pepper
> sauce, smoked oysters, crab meat, smoked
> mussels, spiced octopus, teriaki broiled
> mackerel, retort-packaged smoked salmon,
> and Japanese smoked sauries are just a few
> trout
> 1 cucumber, sliced in rounds and cut in matchsticks
> 1-2 avocados, sliced
> grated ginger
> Japanese pickled vegetables, sliced (they come in
> 4-oz cans and usually contain eggplant, radish,
> bamboo shoots, sword-beans)

for dipping sushi: powdered wasabi (Japanese horseradish) mixed with water or buy pre-mixed wasabi in a small tube
soy sauce to mix with wasabi
toasted sesame seeds

At Home: Package sushi rice in ziploc bag. Put rice vinegar in a nalgene bottle. Put nori in a ziploc. Put fresh produce in paper bags. Pack cans. In a ziploc put a small bottle of soy, toasted sesame seeds in a packet, and tube of wasabi. If you're lucky enough to get smoked fish, package it in brown paper.

In Camp: **1.** Prepare sushi rice: bring 4 cups water to a boil, stir in rice, lower heat and cook covered for 20-30 minutes. When rice is cooked, remove from heat, pour rice vinegar over it, and mix with a fork. **2.** Cut all veggies and fish to "sushi size" and set out buffet style with nori. **3.** Make sushi dip: Mix up the wasabi to a thick paste, then mix with soy sauce and set out in a small cup or bowl with sesame seeds on the side.

Swiss Fondue

Makes 6 servings

2 cups dry white wine
2 garlic cloves, coarsely chopped
12 oz imported Swiss cheese
1 TB cornstarch
3 TB kirsch
salt and pepper
pinch nutmeg
1 loaf French bread, slightly stale is preferable

At Home: If this meal is for the first or second night, grate cheese and toss with cornstarch to coat; package in plastic bag. Otherwise, pack cheese ungrated. Add spices to main supply. Put kirsch in small nalgene bottle. Put white wine in nalgene bottle. Pack bread in a paper bag.

In Camp: **1.** Add garlic cloves to white wine in a pot and bring to a boil. **2.** Let cook for a minute or two and add cheese a handful at a time (if grated in camp, mix cornstarch with cheese). When cheese is all melted and creamy season with salt, pepper and nutmeg and stir in the kirsch. **3.** Cut the French bread into 1-2" cubes and dip into fondue.

Thai Peanut Chicken

Makes 5-6 servings

Full of exotic Thai flavors, this is a hearty yet elegant meal. Use low-salt products or it will be too salty.

1 red or green bell pepper, cut in strips, fresh *or* dehydrated
1 fresh carrot *or* 1 TB dehydrated grated carrot
1 small onion
1 TB safflower oil
Peanut Spice Mix:
    ⅓ cup peanut butter
    2 cloves garlic, minced
    1 jalapeño pepper *or* ¼ tsp red pepper flakes
    ¼ cup soy sauce
    1 tsp grated ginger
    2 lime leaves
    1 bulb end of lemongrass stalk, crushed
14½-oz can whole tomatoes or ½ cup tomato flakes mixed with 1 cup water
50 gram package unsweetened coconut cream powder mixed with 1 cup cold water *or* 12 oz canned coconut milk
Optional: 1 slightly under-baked potato
5-oz can chicken
water to thin
Garnish: lime juice, fresh chopped cilantro

At Home: Combine peanut spice mix and put in nalgene bottle. Add oil to main supply. Package dehydrated vegetables together. Put fresh lime and vegetables in separate brown paper bags. Pack canned chicken and canned tomatoes.

In Camp: 1. Rehydrate dried vegetables. 2. Sauté onion in oil till translucent. Add dehydrated vegetables and Peanut Spice Mix and cook 7 minutes. 3. Add canned tomatoes with their juice or tomato flakes and the potato cut in 2" chunks. Add coconut milk. Gently stir in canned chicken. During this time you may need to add water to thin. Peanut butter burns easily, so watch it carefully. Discard lemongrass bulb. 4. Serve on a bed of rice and garnish with fresh chopped cilantro and lime.

Trout Tarragon

Makes 3 servings

This tarragon-wine sauce makes a trout dinner an elegant meal. Serve the fish surrounded with colorful stir-fried vegetables: carrots, zucchini, snow peas, sweet red pepper strips.

3 frying-pan-sized trout
4 TB butter (real butter, please)
2 cloves garlic, minced
¼ tsp dried tarragon
¾ cup dry white wine
1 tsp fresh parsley, minced
Garnish: lemon wedges and parsley sprigs

At Home: Pack fresh parsley and lemon in separate brown paper bags. Add butter and garlic to main supply. Put wine in a small nalgene bottle and wine in a film can.

In Camp: **1.** Melt 3 TB of butter in skillet over medium heat until it bubbles. Add minced garlic and a pinch of the tarragon and cook for about 10 minutes, or until done (see the recipe for *Bill's Trout* on page 113 for details on how to panfry trout). **2.** When trout are cooked, remove from pan to a warm lplate and cover. Deglaze skillet by adding wine to pan juices and turning heat up to high. Add parsley and the rest of the tarragon. Boil for a minute or so, scraping the residue from sides and bottom of pan. Most of the liquid will boil away and the sauce will thicken a bit. **3.** When sauce has thickened, remove from heat and swirl in the remaining 1 TB of butter. Pour sauce over fish and serve with lemon wedges and parsley sprigs.

Cream of Dilled Salmon

Makes 4 servings

A basic cream sauce can be used to create any number of good meals for backpackers. Creamed tuna, creamed chicken with freeze-dried peas, and creamed chipped beef are easy old favorites. For gourmet dining try cream sauce with sautéed mushrooms and a shot of sherry, or smoked salmon and cream sauce over linguini. Or try the dilled salmon recipe here.

Basic Cream Sauce (makes 1 cup):
   2 TB butter (real butter, please)
   1½-2 TB flour, white or whole wheat
   ¼ cup dry milk combined with water to make 1
      cup
2 6½-oz cans salmon
   sprig of fresh dill, minced or scant ½ tsp dill weed
   Optional garnish: 1 green onion, minced
   lemon wedges

At Home: Pack fresh produce in brown paper bags. Make a spice packet. Pack salmon. Add butter, flour, and dry milk to main supply.

In Camp: **1.** Make Basic Cream Sauce: A wire whisk or a wooden spoon is the best utensil to use. Melt butter over low heat. When it has melted and heated through, slowly blend in flour and cook over low heat for 10 minutes. Then *slowly and gradually* blend in 1 cup of milk and stir till thickened and smooth. Since the white sauce will have a raw flour taste if you serve it too soon, put it on the very lowest simmer, stirring when necessary, while you prepare your pasta, rice, or toast. Add more water if necessary. **2.** Add canned salmon and dill and heat through. A few minutes before serving stir in minced green onion. Serve over rice, pasta, or *Frying Pan Toast* (page 113) with a squeeze of fresh lemon.

Easy Instant Chicken Chili

Makes 4-5 servings

14½-oz can whole or chopped tomatoes
14½-oz can kidney beans
5-oz can chicken
7-oz can tomato salsa
2 TB chili powder
pinch of cloves
½ tsp leaf oregano
dash Tabasco sauce
2 TB masa harina or instant polenta
Garnishes: fresh grated onion, grated cheese

At Home: Combine spices and put in a spice packet. Include small plastic bottle of Tabasco sauce. Make a packet for masa harina or polenta. Pack onion and cheese in brown paper. Pack cans.

In Camp: **1.** Combine all canned foods with their juice and the spices. **2.** Heat through, then stir in masa harina or polenta gradually to thicken. If chili gets too thick you may need to thin it with water. Serve piping hot and garnish with fresh grated onion and cheese if desired.

Yu Shiang Eggplant

Makes 4 servings

You can use fresh ground meat in this spicy Szechuan dish, but backpackers must always keep fresh meat chilled and use it the first night to avoid the dangers of spoilage. You can enjoy this meal after many days on the trail if you use textured vegetable protein. Textured vegetable protein (TVP), makes an excellent meat substitute for backpackers. For more information on TVP, see the glossary.

2 small eggplants cut in rounds and then cut in ½"
    strips, dehydrated (should equal about 3 cups
    dehydrated eggplant)
⅓ cup TVP or ¼ lb ground beef, pork, or turkey
3 green onions, minced
2-4 TB peanut or other oil to sauté eggplant and
    spice mixture

Spice Mixture:
  ¼ tsp red pepper flakes
  1 TB miso paste or 1 packet miso soup (to make
    2 6-oz servings)
  2 cloves garlic, minced
  1 TB soy sauce
  1 tsp sugar
  2 tsp sesame oil
  1 TB grated fresh ginger
Marinade:
  1 tsp cornstarch
  1 TB soy sauce
  1 TB sherry
Optional garnishes: chopped fresh cilantro *or*
  Cilantro-Peanut Oil Pesto (page 179)

At Home: Package dehydrated eggplant in a sealable plastic bag. Package TVP in a plastic bag, or triple-bag ground meat in a plastic bag to prevent leakage and keep chilled till you start hiking. Add oil to main supply. Combine spice mixture in a nalgene bottle. Put marinade ingredients in another bottle. Put green onions in a brown paper bag.

In Camp: 1. Separately rehydrate eggplant and TVP (if you're using it) with boiling water to cover. Mince green onions, including stems. 2. When TVP is rehydrated (about 10 minutes), gently squeeze out excess water. Stir marinade into TVP or ground meat. 3. Press excess rehydrating water out of eggplant and sauté in frying pan over medium high heat for about 10 minutes. Set aside in another pot. 4. Add 1 TB oil to skillet and turn heat to high. Add spice mixture and green onions and stir-fry for about 1 minute. Add meat- or TVP-marinade mixture and stir-fry 2 minutes. Add sautéed eggplant and stir-fry 2 more minutes. Serve hot over rice or oriental noodles with cilantro garnish.

Shrimp Steamed in Beer

Makes 4 servings

I first served this meal on a kayaking trip along the Molokai coast, and it was such a hit that we all had the dunk sauce butter dripping down to our elbows! It's a quick and easy meal in camp—yet awfully extravagant and fun. Shrimp must, of course, be a first night meal.

2 8-oz cans beer
Steaming Spices:
    1 tsp thyme
    1 tsp dry mustard
    2 bay leaves
    4 cloves garlic, minced
    1 tsp salt
    1 TB chopped parsley
    ¼ tsp freshly ground pepper
    1 TB chopped chives or green onion
3 lbs shrimp in their shells
Dunk sauce:
    1 cube butter (real butter, please)
    2 minced garlic cloves
    4 TB lemon juice
    2 TB chopped parsley
    1 TB chopped chives *or* green onions

At Home: 1. Prepare Dunk Sauce: Melt butter, add all other ingredients. Put in a wide mouth nalgene jar. **2.** Put Steaming Spices including minced garlic, and chopped onion together in a spice packet. Pack beer. **3.** Shrimp may be frozen or fresh, but should be in shells. Pack in sealable plastic bags and keep cold till you start hiking.

In Camp: 1. Pour beer into a large cooking pot and add spices. Bring to a boil. As soon as liquid comes to a boil add shrimp. Let shrimp simmer 5 minutes. They should get pink, no more. **2.** Meanwhile, scoop Dunk Sauce into a small cooking pot and melt butter thoroughly taking care not to burn. **3.** Serve shrimps in their shells right in the cooking pot. Everyone peels their own shrimp and dunks them into the butter sauce.

Make-Ahead Meals

These four special feasts are made at home and brought into camp already prepared. Except for cooking things like rice and couscous, all you have to do is heat and eat.

New West Smoked Turkey Breast With Cilantro Sweet Potatoes

Makes 8 servings

Blood Oranges and Capers with Spring-Mix Baby Lettuces *(page 140) makes this a meal fit for royalty.*

> 1 4-lb turkey breast, boned and butterflied
> Marinade:
>> Optional: 1 TB liquid smoke
>> ⅔ cup olive oil
>> ⅓ cup white wine
>> juice of one lemon
>> 1 TB grated ginger
>> 1 tsp tarragon
>> 10 cloves garlic, slivered
>> fresh ground pepper
>> sea salt (Hawaiian salt if you can get it)
> 8 whole sweet potatoes
> *Cilantro-Peanut Oil Pesto* (page 179)

At Home

1. Have your butcher bone and butterfly a turkey breast, it will be about 3-4 inches thick. Don't have it skinned. The skin holds garlic and marinade next to the meat and keeps it moist while cooking, too.
2. Rub turkey with salt and freshly ground pepper. Peel and sliver garlic and insert in turkey into the meat and under skin. This is easy to do because the boning has left many slits where you can insert garlic. Combine remainder of marinade ingredients, rub into turkey breast and under skin. Put in a covered bowl and marinate for 6-12 hours, turning often. 3. Remove from refrigerator about an hour before ready to go on the grill. Barbeque in a Weber-type barbeque if at all possible. When coals are ready (use charcoal and mesquite), place on oiled grill and adjust both bottom and lid vents to

halfway open. Cook for at least an hour, possibly 1½ hours at this medium-low heat adjustment, checking and turning when necessary. Take care not to overcook and dry it out. Use a meat thermometer if necessary. **4.** When turkey breast is cooked, remove from heat and set on a large piece of heavy duty aluminum foil. When it has completely cooled, wrap smoked turkey in two layers of heavy duty aluminum foil and store in refrigerator. **5.** Prepare *Cilantro-Peanut Oil Pesto* and put in a nalgene bottle. Bake sweet potatoes at 350 degrees for about 40 minutes. They should, if anything, be slightly underdone.

In Camp: **1.** Smoked turkey may be served warm or cold. If you wish to heat, leave in foil and put in covered frying pan over low heat until warmed through. **2.** Prepare potatoes: Cut baked potatoes diagonally in 2" widths. Coat frying pan or Banks Frybake Pan thickly with peanut oil and heat potatoes over medium heat. Turn potatoes often. They'll be extra tasty if they brown just a bit. When heated through, garnish with generous dollops of cilantro-peanut oil pesto and serve with thinly sliced smoked turkey.

Cajun Black Beans and Rice

Makes 8 servings

This recipe calls for Andouille sausage, but a spicy poultry sausage would be good, too. For a pull-out-the-stops feast, serve with Shrimp Steamed in Beer *(page 205).*

Beans:
   2 cups black beans
   2 yellow onions, diced
   4 garlic cloves
   2 jalapeño peppers
   3 Anaheim peppers
   2 sweet peppers—red, yellow or green bell
      or pimiento
   1 tsp salt
   ¼ tsp pepper
   2 tsp ground cumin
   2 tsp oregano leaves
   12-16 oz Andouille sausage cut in ¼" rounds
   olive oil
   ¼ -½ cup Marukan seasoned gourmet rice vinegar
Rice:
   2 cups Basmati rice
   4 cups boiling water

At Home: 1. This is nearly the same recipe for dehydrating black beans found in *Chapter 15* so follow the recipe for *Black Beans* on page 165 through Step 2. When the bean liquor is thick and rich, prepare the other ingredients. 2. Cut peppers in half lengthwise. Remove seeds and ribs and thinly slice horizontally. Sauté in olive oil for 5 minutes with onions. Add garlic, spices, and sliced Andouille and cook over medium heat for ten minutes. 3. Add this mixture to beans, reserving half the Andouille. Continue to cook beans for another hour, adjusting the seasonings as you wish. 4. About fifteen minutes before taking beans off heat, stir in remaining Andouille. Add vinegar and cook for 5 minutes. 5. Package in vacuum packaging bags or Seal-A-Meal and refrigerate or freeze. Make two bags if you're bringing the entire recipe, it will be easier to transport. Package 2 cups Basmati rice in vacuum packaging bags or Seal-A-Meal.

In Camp: 1. Heat beans in a cooking pot taking care not to burn them on the bottom. 2. Meanwhile, prepare Basmati rice. Bring 4 cups water to a boil, stir in rice and quickly bring back to boil. Then turn down heat to low simmer, keeping lid on pot for 20-30 minutes. Make a bed of rice for beans and serve.

Spring Lamb Curry and Couscous
Makes 6 serving

Curry travels well because the spices are natural preservatives. You can prepare this ahead of time and freeze it—just be sure it's thawed in time for dinner. For dessert, serve mint tea and, like the Indians, pass a bowl of white sugar and fennel seeds to aid digestion.

3 lbs boneless lamb stew meat, cut in 1-inch cubes
Marinade:
    1 cup plain yogurt
    ¼ tsp red pepper flakes, or to taste
    ½ tsp salt
    ¼ cup ghee (available in Indian grocery stores)
    or **¼ cup oil**
    2 cups chopped onion
    2 TB grated ginger
    5 large cloves garlic, minced
Curry Spices:
    2 tsp crushed coriander seed
    1 tsp crushed cumin seed
    ¼ tsp crushed cardamom seed
    1 tsp ground turmeric
    ½ tsp ground cinnamon
    1 tsp garum masala
Optional: 1-2 TB vindaloo paste (hottest) *or* curry
    paste
1 cup chicken broth
½ cup plain yogurt
2 cups instant couscous
Condiments (see below)

At Home: 1. In a large mixing bowl, combine marinade ingredients, mix with lamb, cover and place in refrigerator stirring occasionally. Marinate for 4-12 hours. 2. In a large pot over medium-high heat, melt ghee or oil. Stir in onion, ginger, garlic, and curry spices.

Cook for 7 minutes or until onion is tender. **3.** Stir yogurt and lamb into ghee and spices. Gradually blend chicken broth into ¼ cup yogurt and add to curry. Bring to boil, reduce heat, cover and simmer until meat is tender, about 2 hours. **4.** Let cool completely. Package in vacuum-packaging bags or Seal-A-Meal and refrigerate or freeze. Make two bags if you're bringing the entire recipe, it will be easier to transport. **5.** Package 2 cups couscous in vacuum-packaging bag or Seal-A-Meal. Package condiments. Keep curry in cooler until you start hiking.

In Camp: **1.** Heat curry and prepare condiments. **2.** Prepare couscous as directed. When it's ready, serve curry on a bed of couscous and set out condiments. Diners spoon condiments onto curry.

Condiments

Just a little taste of each condiment is enough, and you can bring them all or only a few. Most curry lovers feel that chutney is a must.

> **chutney (1 cup at least)**
> **½ cup raisins**
> **⅓ cup chopped peanuts**
> **⅓ cup unsweetened dried coconut**
> **2-3 eggs, hard-boiled and chopped**
> **ginger preserves**
> **sweet pickles**
> **1 or 2 bananas, sliced (bananas cool down a hot mouth)**
> **1 or 2 kiwi fruit, peeled and sliced**

Puttanesca with Goat Cheese And Angel Hair Pasta

Makes 2 servings

This recipe was given to me by Steve Adams, a chef at Berkeley's Ristorante Venezia where this dish is served. Even if you don't like anchovies, they give Puttanesca a piquancy that would be lacking without them.

Puttanesca Base:
  1 cup olive oil
  10-15 cloves garlic, peeled
  1 heaping TB dry basil
  1 tsp red pepper flakes
  ¼ tsp white pepper
  32-36 oz canned Italian plum tomatoes
  ⅓ cup capers
  ½ cup pitted calamata olives
Puttanesca for Two:
  3-5 anchovy fillets, rinsed and patted dry
  2 TB olive oil
  6 oz Puttanesca Base
  4 oz fresh tomatoes, peeled, seeded, and chopped
  1 TB chopped fresh basil
  2 oz goat cheese
  8 oz Angel hair pasta

At Home: 1. Make Puttanesca Base: In a heavy 3-quart pot sauté whole garlic cloves in olive oil over low heat for at least 10 minutes. They should be slightly browned and soft. Add basil, red pepper flakes, white pepper and plum tomatoes. Simmer for 30-45 minutes. Turn heat off. Add capers and olives. This is your base. 2. In a deep skillet sauté anchovy fillets in olive oil till anchovies are broken down. Add Puttanesca Base, tomatoes, and basil. Heat then remove from heat. 3. Freeze remainder of Puttanesca Base for another meal. Package Puttanesca for Two in vacuum package bag or Seal-A-Meal and refrigerate. 4. Put pasta in ziploc. Pack goat cheese and keep in cooler with Puttanesca till you start hiking.

In Camp: Cook pasta and heat Puttanesca. The moment pasta is drained, add sauce and toss and serve immediately with crumbled goat cheese garnish.

17

Desserts

Dessert can be as simple as a piece of fruit or a cup of hot chocolate, but sometimes we want more, and it can be fun to make a fancy dessert in camp. The desserts in this chapter are all cooked, baked or assembled in camp, and range from flaming *Cherries Jubilee* to easy *Girl Scout S'mores*. Most recipes here should satisfy even the most incorrigible sweet tooth. In the **Breads and Baked Goods** chapter you'll find desserts you can make at home: *Mer's Prune Cake, Lemon Loaf Cake, Madeline's Jam Squares, Peggy's Date Bars,* and *Camper's Coffeecake.*

Cherries Jubilee

Makes 6 servings

This flaming dessert is impressive, yet simple—once you know how to do it. If you've never made a flaming dessert before, it's a good idea to read over the recipe and get the game plan fixed in your mind before lighting the match.

6-8 oz dried sweet cherries *or* **one 14½-oz can pitted Bing cherries**
2 TB cornstarch
2 TB sugar
¼ cup warmed kirsch
6 pieces of chocolate

At Home: Package dried cherries in a boilable plastic bag. Package sugar and cornstarch together in a plastic bag. Put kirsch in a nalgene bottle. Pack chocolate.

In Camp: **1.** Rehydrate the cherries in 1 cup of boiling water for at least 30 minutes—an hour would be better. Drain cherries and set aside liquid. **2.** When the cherries are rehydrated, combine cornstarch-sugar and rehydrating liquid. Mix in liquid a little at a time so it won't lump. Cook in a frying pan over medium-high heat till it thickens. If the sauce gets too thick, add a little water. Then add cherries and heat through. **3.** Heat the kirsch in a small pot. This can be tricky. If it boils, all the alcohol will evaporate and it won't flame—or if the alcohol gets too hot it can ignite spontaneously. On the other hand, if you don't heat it enough, it may not ignite at all. When the kirsch is *hot* but not boiling it's at ignition temperature. **4.** Have your matches ready. Gently pour the kirsch all over the cherries, light it, and stir while it's flaming. Blue and gold flames will be dripping from the spoon as you dish it into individual bowls over the chocolate pieces.

Chocolate-Almond Brownies

Makes 8 servings

A few of the supermarket brownie mixes are pretty good, but not like these. Because brownies must be baked at high heat, the steaming method won't work. Use the mini-oven method.

½ **cup slivered almonds, toasted and chopped**
⅓ **cup sugar**
¾ **cup flour**
½ **cup powdered egg (or powder to equal 2 eggs)**
¼ **tsp baking soda**
¼ **tsp salt**
¾ **cup water**
2 **TB butter**
12 **oz semi-sweet chocolate chips**
⅓ **tsp almond extract (don't use more than this)**

At Home: 1. Toast almonds in a small frying pan over medium heat till light brown. When almonds have cooled completely put them in a food processor, and finely chop. Then put them in a small plastic bag, including both nut powder and finely chopped nuts. 2. Combine sugar, flour, powdered egg, baking soda, and salt in a ziploc. Pack chocolate chips and almond extract in a small nalgene bottle. Add butter to main supply.

In Camp: 1. In a 3-quart pot combine water, butter, and half the chocolate chips and stir constantly over medium-low heat till chocolate is melted. 2. Remove from heat, add flour mixture, and stir till blended. Add almonds, almond extract, and the rest of the chocolate chips. 3. Pour into a well-oiled Banks Frybake Pan (or equivalent) and bake with stove on simmer and a twig fire on top for 30 minutes or more. Allow to cool and cut into squares.

Strawberry Shortcake

Makes 6 servings

Because shortcake biscuits must be baked at high heat, use the mini-oven method.

⅓ cup whole wheat flour
½ cup sifted white flour
1 ½ tsp baking powder
¼ tsp salt
¼ tsp cream of tartar
1 ½ TB sugar
3 TB soft butter
¼ cup dry milk mixed with ½ cup water
Strawberry Sauce (see below)

At Home: Combine ingredients in a plastic bag. Add butter to main supply.

In Camp: **1.** Cut butter into dry ingredients. In camp you can use two knives or rub lumps between your fingers till dough is about the consistency of course cornmeal. **2.** Add milk all at once and stir dough vigorously for just barely a minute. Add more water if necessary to blend ingredients, but stir as little as possible. **3.** Form into 6 balls, flatten to 1½" thick, and put into a lightly-oiled Banks Frybake Pan (or equivalent), setting cakes as far apart as room allows. **4.** Bake for at least 15 minutes with stove on simmer and twig fire on top. Serve warm with *Strawberry Sauce*, preserves, or stewed fruit.

Strawberry Sauce

Dried strawberries are quite fragile, so treat them gently.

2 cups dried *or* freeze-dried strawberries
hot water to cover
1 TB cornstarch
1 TB sugar

At Home: Package cornstarch and sugar together in a plastic packet. Put strawberries in a ziploc and pack in a cooking pot for protection.

In Camp: **1.** Rehydrate strawberries by covering them with hot, but not boiling water. When berries are soft, drain the hydrating water into a frying pam and over medium heat gradually blend in cornstarch-sugar mixture, taking care not to let lumps form. **2.** Cook till thickened; add more water if necessary to thin. Gently stir in berries and heat through. Spoon over warm shortcake and serve.

Girl Scout S'mores

Makes 1 serving

If you indulge in an occasional trip to junk food land, S'mores are just the ticket. They're high-fat, high-sugar, high-calorie, and almost completely lacking in nutritional value. My only problem with S'mores is that marshmallows aren't what they used to be. I distinctly remember roasted marshmallows which, taffy-like, pulled away from the stick in a long string down onto your chin and shirt as you popped them into your mouth. Today's marshmallows don't do that. They don't get as gooey as in the olden days, and they disappear in your hot chocolate. Nevertheless, they will do in this recipe.

1 marshmallow
4 chocolate Hershey-bar squares
2 Graham crackers

In Camp:

Toast a marshmallow on a stick over the flame of your camp stove. Place chocolate on one graham cracker. Top chocolate with marshmallow, and cover with second cracker to form a sandwich.

Pear Torte

Makes 6 servings

2 TB flour
¼ cup sugar
¼ cup powdered egg
1 tsp baking powder
¼ tsp salt
½ cup chopped walnuts
2 canned pears, cut in 1-inch chunks or 3 oz dried
    pears
1 tsp vanilla extract
⅓ cup water
2 tsp butter for preparing pan

At Home: Sift together flour, sugar, powdered egg, baking powder and salt. Put into sealable plastic bag. Put walnuts into another plastic bag. If using dried pears package in a boilable plastic bag. Bring a small nalgene container of vanilla.

In Camp: **1.** Rehydrate pears if using dried pears. **2.** Stir water into flour mixture and beat well. Stir in pears, nuts and vanilla until just blended. **3.** Butter Banks Frybake Pan (or equivalent) well and pour batter in. Cover and make a twig fire with coals on lid. Set stove at low simmer; make good hot coals on top for this recipe. Bake 30 minutes. Torte should be thin and crispy.

Nightcap Apricots

Makes 4 servings

This is your basic recipe for stewing dried fruit; the apricot brandy enhances the taste of the apricots. Try stewing any dried fruit, just plain or with added spices or with a small piece of lemon or orange peel. Put stewed fruit on breakfast cereal, use as a jam on biscuits, or as a dessert sauce for shortcake.

2 cups dried apricots
boiling water to cover
Optional: 2 shots apricot brandy

At Home: Package ingredients.

In Camp: **1.** Pour boiling water over dried apricots. They'll take less time to stew if you let them rehydrate for an hour or so before putting on the stove. **2.** Simmer on stove, and when apricots are soft and ready to serve, stir in apricot brandy.

Variation: Try cinnamon, sugar, and apple brandy with dried apples.

Your Wildest Dreams Popcorn

Makes 3 pots popcorn

*Eating nutritional yeast is supposed to discourage mos-
quitos and other insects from going after you. I'm also
told that it will give you vivid dreams. In any case, it
tastes good on popcorn.*

1 cup popcorn
6 TB oil for popping
⅔ cup nutritional yeast
sea salt

At Home: Package ingredients.

In Camp: **1.** You will pop the corn in three batches to prevent
burning. Put 2 TB oil and ⅓ cup popcorn in a frying
pan or heavy bottomed pot. Cover and heat at
medium high till it pops, shaking pan constantly. **2.**
When popcorn has popped, sprinkle nutritional
yeast over it while it's hot.

Variations: Try dressing up popcorn with Parmesan cheese, Tamari, Spike, garlic salt, maple syrup,
or honey.

"Weight Watcher's" Cheesecake

Makes 1 small pie, about 6 servings

This is surely not the way Weight Watcher's intended their low-calorie cheesecake mousse to be eaten, but this excellent instant mix is perfect for the backpacker hungering for a luscious dessert.

2 1.45-oz packages of Weight Watcher's Cheesecake Mousse
½ cup dry milk
10 oz cold water
1 prepared Graham cracker piecrust

At Home: Package dry milk in ziploc. Pack cheescake mix packages. Pack piecrust in a cooking pot or some safe place in your pack where it won't break.

In Camp: **1.** Prepare Cheesecake Mousse: Pour cold water into a cooking pot, add mix and dry milk, and whip with a wire whisk for a few minutes. **2.** Scrape thickened cheesecake mousse into piecrust and serve.

Hazelnut Chocolate Mousse à la Weight Watchers

Makes 2 servings

Yet another way for hungry campers to pack those fine Weight Watcher's desserts chock full of calories.

1.45-oz package Weight Watcher's Chocolate Mousse
scant ¼ cup dry milk
5 oz cold water
¼ cup shavings of Lindt Hazelnut Chocolate Bar

At Home: Pack Mousse packet and dry milk in a plastic bag.

In Camp: **1.** Prepare Chocolate Mousse: Pour cold water into a cooking pot, add mix and dry milk, and whip with a wire whisk for a few minutes. **2.** When mousse has thickened, gently fold in hazelnut chocolate shavings.

Variations: Fold in 2 TB Kahlua, brandy, or Irish whiskey.

Glossary

If you can't find what you're looking for in the glossary, it's probably defined somewhere else in the book. Check the index for the page number.

ANDOUILLE SAUSAGE A spicy hot pork sausage originally used in southern cooking. Shrimp and Andouille are a classic combination in Creole southern cooking.

BALSAMIC VINEGAR An outrageously good imported Italian vinegar made from Modena grapes and aged in wood barrels. Expensive, but worth it.

BEAN CURD See *Tofu*

BLOOD ORANGE An orange with blood-red flesh found in specialty produce markets. Good in salads with a vinaigrette dressing. Regular oranges can be substituted.

BULGUR WHEAT Precooked cracked wheat. An outstanding backpacking food because it's nutritious, delicious, and filling, and cooks in only 15 minutes. Can be used as a dinner pilaf, in a grain salad, or as a breakfast cereal.

CALAMATA OLIVE A salty, highly flavorful black olive sold in gourmet and specialty food shops.

CHUTNEY An Indian relish usually served with curries. Chutneys are commonly made with onions, vinegar, sugar, fruit, chilies, and ginger. They're usually salty and spicy. Major Grey's, a popular brand with Americans, can be found in many supermarkets.

CORNICHONS Little sweet pickles usually found in gourmet markets.

COUSCOUS A grainlike pasta made from durum wheat, the national dish of the Magreb people of Morocco, Algeria, and Tunisia. Couscous is sold in health-food stores and Middle Eastern markets. Be certain to get only the instant variety for backpacking. Couscous can be used like rice or as a breakfast cereal, and comes in both white and whole wheat varieties.

FISH SAUCE Used like soy sauce in much of southeast Asia. A dark, salty liquid, it's made from salted anchovies. Quality varies greatly, so get the most expensive brand. Available in Thai groceries.

GALANGA A rhizome (root-like plant), also known as Thai ginger although ginger is not a substitute for it. It's used in the Thai Tom Yum soup recipe. Sold fresh in Thai markets, and also sold dried in slices or powdered. Always buy it fresh.

GHEE Clarified butter. It has a higher burning point than butter because the milk solids are discarded when Ghee is prepared. It's traditionally preferred to butter in many Indian recipes and is available in large jars in Indian groceries. Ghee is a good choice for backpackers going on very long trips because it can keep for months without refrigeration. Salted butter can keep for backpacking trips of up to ten days without refrigeration.

GINGER A rhizome, comes fresh, candied, or powdered. Powdered and fresh ginger are widely available in supermarkets. Use fresh ginger when called for in these recipes. Candied ginger is sugar-coated and chewy with a texture something like gumdrops. You can find it in some supermarkets, health-food stores, and Asian markets. Powdered ginger is not a satisfactory substitute. Fresh ginger is good for settling upset stomachs.

HALVAH A confection of Turkish origin made with honey and sesame seeds.

HUMMUS Made from garbanzo flour, tahini, lemon, and garlic. Mixes are sold in health-food stores and are quite good. Instant hummus makes a good lunch or snack dip with pita bread or fresh vegetables. The taste of the mixes can be improved with lots of lemon juice and a sprinkling of olive oil and parsley.

JICAMA A legume that grows underground as a tuber and is used extensively in Mexican cooking. It has a thick brown outer skin and a sweet, crunchy flesh something like a potato. It stays fresh indefinitely, and can be used in salads on the trail, as a substitute for water chestnuts in stir-fries, and as a fresh vegetable to dip in salsa.

LEMONGRASS An essential ingredient that has a lemony-floral flavor and is used in many southeast Asian dishes including the *Thai Peanut Chicken* and *Thai Tom Yum* soup recipes. It's available in health-food stores, large produce markets, and Asian markets. To use as a spice in these recipes, pull off a couple of the stalks and cut off the coarse, grass-like ends. Crush bulb end and add to recipe. The plant is too coarse to eat, so remove before serving. A refreshing tea can be made from lemongrass, too. Pour boiling water over the crushed bulb ends.

MASA HARINA A finely ground cornmeal used in Mexican cooking. Use masa harina to make tortillas or thicken chili beans. Widely available in the Mexican section in California supermarkets and in Mexican groceries.

MEDJOOL DATE A large, moist, delicious date far superior to the dry dates sold in boxes in supermarkets; found in the produce section of specialty produce markets. Regular dates can be substituted.

MISO A paste made from cooked, fermented soy beans. There are various types—red, white, brownish, and beige. They vary in strength and saltiness and are used as a base in miso soup. Available in health-food stores and Oriental markets. A little goes a long way.

MUSCAT RAISIN A delicious raisin made from the muscat grape. Muscat raisins can be found in Italian groceries and sometimes in supermarkets.

MUSHROOMS Mushrooms are a boon to back-packers because they taste even better when they're dehydrated, they add wonderful flavor to soups and sauces, and they will last for days when packed fresh in a brown paper bag. Most of us are familiar with the supermarket commercial mush-rooms, but you may want to visit a specialty pro-duce market and try other varieties. Shiitake, or black forest, mushrooms have a wonderful meaty taste. Chantrelles are a bright yellow, trumpet-shaped mushroom with a scent of apricot and a wonderful delicate flavor. Hedgehogs, cepes and morels are all exceptionally good, lightweight mushrooms for backpacking gourmets.

NUTRITIONAL YEAST High in B vitamins, nu-tritional yeast is sold in powder or flakes and is widely available in health-food stores. It can be stirred into dry milk or juice as an energizing morn-ing drink, or added to bread or mixed into cereal to boost their nutritional value. It's also good sprin-kled on popcorn.

ORIENTAL SESAME OIL There are two kinds of sesame oil: the cold-pressed cooking oil made from raw sesame seeds and sold in health-food stores, and the oriental oil made from toasted sesame seeds which is used as a strong flavoring agent rather than as a cooking oil. All recipes calling for sesame oil in this book are for oriental sesame oil. Add after cooking, as its smoky flavor is destroyed by heat. Available in Asian groceries and in the specialty section of some supermarkets.

PEANUT OIL The recipes in this book that call for peanut oil mean a high-quality, fragrant, cold-pressed peanut oil, not the cheaper kind used mainly for deep-fat frying.

POLENTA Polenta may be indelicately called cornmeal mush. In fact, it's a traditional Italian dish which is becoming more and more popular in con-temporary American gourmet cuisine. It's an ideal food for backpackers. It can be eaten at dinner in place of rice, pasta, or potatoes or as a cereal at breakfast. If allowed to cool and become firm, it can be cut into bars and fried. There are coarse and fine polenta flours—and instant polenta which takes only five minutes to cook. Backpackers should get the instant polenta. It's available in some health-food stores and in gourmet markets.

PROSCIUTTO Italian ham. It's delicious chopped into pasta cream sauces or as a lunch meat. Wrap a piece of cantaloupe in sliced prosciutto and eat for breakfast or dinner hors d'oeuvres.

RICE VINEGAR All recipes in this book calling for rice vinegar are for Marukan seasoned gourmet rice vinegar. It contains a little sugar and salt and is reduced to 4.1 acidity with water. Regular rice vinegar is quite a different thing and not a satisfactory substitute.

SNOW PEAS Edible podded peas (as opposed to shelling peas) that are available in supermarkets or Asian markets. They are an excellent backpacking vegetable because they are light weight and stay fresh for days without refrigeration. Snow peas take only a couple of minutes to cook, and go in just about any dish. They're best when cooked only to a crunchy stage.

SUN-DRIED TOMATOES Dehydrated tomatoes dried in the sun. Some people eat them plain, but most prefer them rehydrated and added to tomato sauces or sautéed with herbs, spices, garlic and olive oil and spread on bread or eaten over pasta. To rehydrate sun-dried tomatoes, cover with boiling water, cover, and set aside for about 30 minutes—longer if you want softer tomatoes for making tomato sauce.

TAHINI A Middle Eastern spread made from ground, unhulled sesame seeds. Sold in jars in health-food stores, raw or roasted, and can be used like peanut butter or as an ingredient in hummus.

TAMARI A rich and flavorful soy sauce. Regular soy sauce can be used as a substitute.

TEXTURED VEGETABLE PROTEIN Also known as TVP, textured vegetable protein is soy in granule form. It can be added to spaghetti sauce, bread, or cereal to boost protein content. It can also be rehydrated, then sautéed, and used in dishes as a meat substitute.

TOFU Also called bean curd, tofu is made from soy beans and is a complete protein. It comes in four forms practical for backpackers: powdered, dried, vacuum-packed, and jerky.

Powdered tofu must be cooked, then a thickener is added and it's left to gel. Make sure you can stand the taste before you carry it into the wilderness with you. It's not very good. Dried tofu must be rehydrated, and its flavor can be improved by cooking it with soy sauce and other oriental flavorings. Vacuum-packed tofu is by far the best; it's ready to eat, yet non-perishable. Unfortunately it's rather heavy. Tofu jerky is made by Wildwood Natural Foods in Marin County, California, and is an excellent, high protein, non-perishable snack for backpackers.

WHEAT GERM Embryo of the wheat berry, high in B vitamins. It can be added to cereals, breads, nut butters, and sauces to boost nutritional value. Wheat germ is widely available in both supermarkets and health-food stores. It comes in both raw and toasted forms. Toasted wheat germ tastes better to most people, but is not quite as nutritious as raw wheat germ.

Mail-Order Sources

The Banks Frybake Pan for baking breads:

> BANKS FRYBAKE COMPANY
> PO Box 183
> Claverock, NY 12513
> (518) 851-7784
> (518) 851-7115

The FoodSaver vacuum-packaging machine:

> THE CABLE KITCHEN
> 340 Townsend Street
> San Francisco, CA 94107
> (800) 842-3001

The Harvest Maid food dehydrator:

> HARVEST MAID
> Alternative Pioneering Systems, Inc.
> 4064 Peavey Road
> Chaska, MN 55318
> (800) 624-2949

Stoves, cooking pots, the BakePacker, food dehydrators, freeze-dried food, all kinds of camping equipment and clothing:

> REI
> PO Box 88125
> Seattle, WA 98138-2125
> (800) 426-4840
>
> CAMPMOR
> 810 Route 17 North
> PO Box 997-E
> Paramus, NJ 97653-0997
> (800) 526-4784

Freeze-dried food:

> ALPINEAIRE
> PO Box 926
> Nevada City, CA 95959
> (800) 322-MEAL

Seaweed trail snacks, Nori-sesame seasoning, and so on:

> RISING TIDE SEA VEGETABLES
> PO Box 1914
> Mendocino, CA 95460
> (707) 937-2109

Refried beans, Nature's Burger, Basmati rice, couscous, etc:

You must order in quantity, but you can write or call to find out where their products are sold:

FANTASTIC FOODS, INC.
106 Galli Drive
Novato, CA 94949
Telephone: (415) 883-7718
FAX: (415) 883-5129

Specialty sausages (Andouille, Chicken-Apple, etc.):

AIDELL'S SAUSAGE COMPANY
1575 Minnesota Street
San Francisco, CA 94107
(415) 285-6660

Smoked meats and jerky:

MEADOW FARMS COUNTRY SMOKEHOUSE
PO Box 1387
Bishop, CA 93514
(619) 873-5311

Tofu jerky:

WILDWOOD NATURAL FOODS
PO Box 939
Fairfax, CA 94930
(415) 459-3919

Authentic Thai and Oriental food:

ERAWAN MARKET
1474-76 University Avenue
Berkeley, CA 94702
(415) 849-9707

Instant polenta, cheeses, all kinds of gourmet food items.

EURO-MARKET
1601 Martin Luther King Way
Berkeley, CA 94709
(415) 841-7737

Ghee, quick-cooking lentils, chutneys, all kinds of Indian food:

BAZAAR OF INDIA
1810 University Avenue
Berkeley, CA 94707
(415) 548-4110

Index

About the author:

Raised in the Sierra foothills, Carole Latimer is from an old pioneer family in the California gold country and has backpacked all her life. In 1978 she founded Outdoor Woman's School/Call of the Wild, which offers hiking and backpacking trips for women to many western places. She leads many of these trips herself, and of course does the cooking.

Call of the Wild, founded by Carole Latimer in 1978, offers hiking and backpacking trips for women to Hawaii, the Southwest, and the High Sierra. Call of the Wild trips emphasize low-impact camping and aim to give participants a deep concern for the future of planet earth. Trips are for beginners through advanced hikers, and feature home-cooked meals prepared with fresh herbs, fruits, vegetables, and home-canned goods from the Latimer family garden and orchard in the Sierra gold country. For more information write Call of the Wild, 2519 Cedar Street, Berkeley, CA 94708.